THE SUBMARINE BOYS AND THE MIDDIES

OR

The Prize Detail at Annapolis

Victor G. Durham

1st WORLD LIBRARY Literary Society

The Submarine Boys and the Middies

Victor G. Durham

© 1st World Library, 2006
PO Box 2211
Fairfield, IA 52556
www.1stworldlibrary.com
First Edition

LCCN: 2006907738

Softcover ISBN: 1-4218-2461-2
Hardcover ISBN: 1-4218-2361-6
eBook ISBN: 1-4218-2561-9

Purchase *"The Submarine Boys and the Middies"*
as a traditional bound book at:
www.1stWorldLibrary.com/purchase.asp?ISBN=1-4218-2461-2

1st World Library is a literary, educational organization
dedicated to:

- Creating a free internet library of downloadable ebooks

- Hosting writing competitions and offering book
  publishing scholarships.

Interested in more 1st World Library books?
contact: literacy@1stworldlibrary.com
Check us out at: www.1stworldlibrary.com

1ˢᵗ World Library Literary Society

Giving Back to the World

"If you want to work on the core problem, it's early school literacy."

- James Barksdale, former CEO of Netscape

"No skill is more crucial to the future of a child, or to a democratic and prosperous society, than literacy."

- Los Angeles Times

Literacy... means far more than learning how to read and write... The aim is to transmit... knowledge and promote social participation."

- UNESCO

"Literacy is not a luxury, it is a right and a responsibility. If our world is to meet the challenges of the twenty-first century we must harness the energy and creativity of all our citizens."

- President Bill Clinton

"Parents should be encouraged to read to their children, and teachers should be equipped with all available techniques for teaching literacy, so the varying needs and capacities of individual kids can be taken into account."

- Hugh Mackay

CONTENTS

CHAPTER I

THE PRIZE DETAIL

"The United States Government doesn't appear very anxious to claim its property, does it, sir?" asked Captain Jack Benson.

The speaker was a boy of sixteen, attired in a uniform much after the pattern commonly worn by yacht captains. The insignia of naval rank were conspicuously absent.

"Now, that I've had the good luck to sell the 'Pollard' to the Navy," responded Jacob Farnum, principal owner of the shipbuilding yard, "I'm not disposed to grumble if the Government prefers to store its property here for a while."

Yet the young shipbuilder - he was a man in his early thirties, who had inherited this shipbuilding business from his father - allowed his eyes to twinkle in a way that suggested there was something else behind his words.

Jack Benson saw that twinkle, but he did not ask questions. If the shipbuilder knew more than he was prepared to tell, it was not for his young captain to ask for information that was not volunteered.

The second boy present, also in uniform, Hal Hastings by name, had not spoken in five minutes. That was like Hal. *He* was the engineer of the submarine torpedo boat, "Pollard." Jack was captain of the same craft, and could do all the talking.

Jacob Farnum sat back, sideways, at his rolltop desk. On top of the desk lay stacked a voluminous though neat pile of papers, letters, telegrams and memoranda that some rival builders of submarine torpedo boats might have been willing to pay much for the privilege of examining. For, at the present moment, there was fierce competition in the air between rival American builders of submarine fighting craft designed for the United States Navy. Even foreign builders and inventors were clamoring for recognition. Yet just now the reorganized Pollard Submarine Boat Company stood at the top of the line. It had made the last sale to the United States Navy Department.

At this moment, out in the little harbor that was a part of the shipyard, the "Pollard" rode gently at anchor. She was the first submarine torpedo boat built at this yard, after the designs of David Pollard, the inventor, a close personal friend of Jacob Farnum.

Moreover, the second boat, named the "Farnum," had just been launched and put in commission, ready at an hour's notice to take the sea in search of floating enemies of the United States.

"The United States will take its boat one of these days, Captain," Mr. Farnum continued, after lighting a cigar. "By the way, did Dave tell you the name we are thinking of for the third boat, now on the stocks?"

"Dave" was Mr. Pollard, the inventor of the Pollard Submarine boat.

"No, sir," Captain Jack replied.

"We have thought," resumed Mr. Farnum, quietly, after blowing out a ring of smoke, "of calling the third boat, now building, the 'Benson.'"

"The - the - what, sir?" stammered Jack, flushing and rising.

"Now, don't get excited, lad," laughed the shipbuilder.

"But - but - naming a boat for the United States Navy after me, sir -"

Captain Jack's face flushed crimson.

"Of course, if you object - " smiled Mr. Farnum, then paused.

"Object? You know I don't, sir. But I am afraid the idea is going to my head," laughed Jack, his face still flushed. "The very idea of there being in the United States Navy a fine and capable craft named after me -"

"Oh, if the Navy folks object," laughed Farnum, "then they'll change the name quickly enough. You understand, lad, the names we give to our boats last only until the craft are sold. The Navy people can change those names if they please."

"It will be a handsome compliment to me, Mr. Farnum. More handsome than deserved, I fear."

"Deserved, well enough," retorted the shipbuilder. "Dave Pollard and I are well enough satisfied that, if it hadn't been for you youngsters, and the superb way in which you handled our first boat, Dave and I would still be sitting on the anxious bench in the ante-rooms of the Navy Department at Washington."

"Well, I don't deserve to have a boat named after me any more than Hal does, or Eph Somers."

"Give us time, won't you, Captain?" pleaded Jacob Farnum, his face straight, but his eyes laughing. "We expect to build at least five boats. If we didn't, this yard never would have been fitted for the present work, and you three boys, who've done so handsomely by us, wouldn't each own, as you now do, ten shares of stock in this company. Never fear; there'll be a 'Hastings' and a 'Somers' added to our fleet one of these days -

The Submarine Boys and the Middies   9

even though some of our boats have to be sold to foreign governments."

"If a boat named the 'Hastings' were sold to some foreign government," laughed Jack Benson, "Hal, here, wouldn't say much about it. But call a boat named the 'Somers,' after Eph, and then sell it, say, to the Germans or the Japanese, and all of Eph's American gorge would come to the surface. I'll wager he'd scheme to sink any submarine torpedo boat, named after him, that was sold to go under a foreign flag."

"I hope we'll never have to sell any of our boats to foreign governments," replied Jacob Farnum, earnestly. "And we won't either, if the United States Government will give us half a show."

"That's just the trouble," grumbled Hal Hastings, breaking into the talk, at last. "Confound it, why don't the people of this country run their government more than they do? Four-fifths of the inventors who get up great things that would put the United States on top, and keep us there, have to go abroad to find a market for their inventions! If I could invent a cannon to-day that would give all the power on earth to the nation owning it, would the American Government buy it from me? No, sir! I'd have to sell the cannon to England, Germany or Japan - or else starve while Congress was talking of doing something about it in the next session. Mr. Farnum, you have the finest, and the only real submarine torpedo boat. Yet, if you want to go on building and selling these craft, you'll have to dispose of most of them abroad."

"I hope not," responded the shipbuilder, solemnly.

Having said his say, Hal subsided. He was likely not to speak again for an hour. As a class, engineers, having to listen much to noisy machinery, are themselves silent.

It was well along in the afternoon, a little past the middle of October. For our three young friends, Jack, Hal and Eph, things were dull just at the present moment. They were drawing their salaries from the Pollard company, yet of late there had been little for them to do.

Yet the three submarine boys knew that big things were in the air. David Pollard was away, presumably on important business. Jacob Farnum was not much given to speaking of plans until he had put them through to the finish. Some big deal was at present "on" with the Government. That much the submarine boys knew by intuition. They felt, therefore, that, at any moment, they were likely to be called into action - to be called upon for big things.

As Jack and Hal sat in the office, silent, while Jacob Farnum turned to his desk to scan one of the papers lying there, the door opened. A boy burst in, waving a yellow envelope.

"Operator said to hustle this wire to you," shouted the boy, panting a bit. "Said it might be big news for Farnum. So I ran all the way."

Jacob Farnum took the yellow envelope, opening it and glancing hastily through the contents.

"It *is* pretty good news," assented the shipbuilder, a smile wreathing his face. "This is for you, messenger."

"This" proved to be a folded dollar bill. The messenger took the money eagerly, then demanded, more respectfully:

"Any answer, sir?"

"Not at this moment, thank you," replied Mr. Farnum. "That is all; you may go, boy."

Plainly the boy who had brought the telegram was disappointed over not getting some inkling of the secret. All Dunhaven, in fact, was wildly agog over any news that affected the Farnum yard. For, though the torpedo boat building industry was now known under the Pollard name, after the inventor of these boats, the yard itself still went under the Farnum name that young Farnum had inherited from his father.

While Jacob Farnum is reading the despatch carefully, for a better understanding, let us speak for a moment of Captain Jack Benson and his youthful comrades and chums.

Readers of the first volume in this series, "The Submarine Boys on Duty," remember how Jack Benson and Hal Hastings strayed into the little seaport town of Dunhaven one hot summer day, and how they learned that it was here that the then unknown but much-talked-about Pollard submarine was being built. Both Jack and Hal had been well trained in machine shops; they had spent much time aboard salt water power craft, and so felt a wild desire to work at the Farnum yard, and to make a study of submarine craft in general.

How they succeeded in getting their start in the Farnum yard, every reader of the preceding volumes knows; how, too, Eph Somers, a native of Dunhaven, managed to "cheek" his way aboard the craft after she had been launched, and how he had always since managed to remain there.

Our same older readers will remember the thrilling experiences of this boyish trio during the early trials of the new submarine torpedo boat, both above and below the surface. These readers will remember, also, for instance, the great prank played by the boys on the watch officer of one of the stateliest battleships of the Navy.

Readers of the second volume, "The Submarine Boys' Trial Trip," will recall, among other things, the desperate efforts made by George Melville, the capitalist, aided by the latter's disagreeable son, Don, to acquire stealthy control of the submarine building company, and their efforts to oust Jack, Hal and Eph from their much-prized employment. These readers will remember how Jack and his comrades spoiled the

Melville plans, and how Captain Jack and his friends handled the "Pollard" so splendidly, in the presence of a board of Navy officers, that the United States Government was induced to buy that first submarine craft.

After that sale, each of the three boys received, in addition to his regular pay, a bank account of a thousand dollars and ten shares of stock in the new company. Moreover, Messrs. Farnum and Pollard had felt wholly justified in promising these talented, daring, hustling submarine boys an assured and successful future.

Jacob Farnum at last looked up from the final reading of the telegram in his hands. Captain Jack Benson's gaze was fixed on his employer's face. Hal Hastings was looking out of a window, with almost a bored look in his eyes.

"You young men wanted action," announced Mr. Farnum, quietly. "I think you'll get it."

"Soon?" questioned Jack, eagerly.

"Immediately, or a minute or two later," laughed the shipbuilder.

"I'm ready," declared Captain Jack, rising.

"It'll take you a little time to hear about it all and digest it, so you may as well be seated again," declared Farnum.

Hal, too, wandered back to his chair.

"You've been wondering how much longer the Government would leave the 'Pollard' here," went on Mr. Farnum. "I am informed that the gunboat 'Hudson' is on her way here, to take over the 'Pollard.'"

"What are the Navy folks going to do?" demanded Captain Jack, all but wrathfully. "Do they propose to *tow* that splendid little craft away?"

"Hardly that, I imagine," replied Farnum. "It's the custom of the United States Navy, you know, to send a gunboat along with every two or three submarines. They call the larger craft the 'parent boat.' The parent boat looks out for any submarine craft that may become disabled."

"The cheek of it," vented Jack, disgustedly. "Why, sir, I'd volunteer to take the 'Pollard,' unassisted, around the world, if she could carry fuel enough for such a trip."

"But the Navy hasn't been accustomed to such capable submarine boats as ours, you know," replied Mr. Farnum. "Hence the parent boat."

"Parent boat?" interjected Hal Hastings, with his quiet smile. "You might call it the 'Dad' boat, so to speak."

Mr. Farnum laughed, then continued:

"A naval crew will take possession of the 'Pollard,' and the craft will proceed, under the care of the Dad boat" - with a side glance of amusement at Hal - "to the United States Naval Academy at Annapolis."

"Annapolis - where they train the naval cadets, the midshipmen, into United States Naval officers? Oh, how I'd like to go there!" breathed Captain Jack Benson, eagerly.

"As a cadet in the Navy, do you mean?" asked Mr. Farnum.

"Why, that would have been well enough," assented Jack, "before I had such a chance in your submarine service. No; I mean I'd like to see Annapolis. I'd like to watch the midshipmen at their training, and see the whole naval life there."

"It's too bad every fellow can't have his wish gratified as easily," continued Jacob Farnum.

"Do you mean we're going to Annapolis, too?" asked Jack Benson, his eyes glowing. Even Hal Hastings sat up straighter in his chair, watching the shipbuilder's face closely.

"Yes," nodded Jacob Farnum. "Permission has been granted for me to send our second boat, the 'Farnum,' along with the 'Pollard' - both under the care of the -"

"The Dad boat," laughed Hastings.

"Yes; that will give us a chance to have the 'Farnum' studied most closely by some of the most capable officers in the United States Navy. It ought to mean, presently, the sale of the 'Farnum' to the Government."

"That's just what it will mean," promised Captain Jack, "if any efforts of ours can make the Navy men more interested in the boat."

"You three youngsters are likely to be at Annapolis for some time," went on Mr. Farnum. "In fact - but don't let your heads become too enlarged by the news, will you?"

Hal, quiet young Hal, neatly hid a yawn behind one hand, while Benson answered for both:

"We're already wearing the largest-sized caps manufactured, Mr. Farnum. Don't tempt us too far, please!"

"Oh, you boys are safe from the ordinary perils of vanity, or your heads would have burst long ago. Well, then, when you arrive at Annapolis, you three are to act as civilian instructors to the middies. You three are to teach the midshipmen of the United States Navy the principles on which the Pollard type of boat is run. There; I've told you the whole news. What do you think of it?"

Mr. Farnum's cigar having burned low, he tossed it away, then leaned back as he lighted another weed.

"What do we think, sir?" echoed Captain Jack, eagerly. "Why, we think we're in sight of the very time of our lives! Annapolis! And to teach the middies how to run a 'Pollard' submarine."

"How soon are we likely to have to start, sir!" asked Hal Hastings, after a silence that lasted a few moments.

"Whenever the 'Hudson' shows up along this coast, and the officer in command of her gives the word. That may be any hour, now."

"Then we'd better find Eph," suggested Captain Jack, "and pass him the word. Won't Eph Somers dance a jig for delight, though?"

"Yes; we'd better look both boats over at once," replied Mr. Farnum, picking up his hat. "And we'll leave word for Grant Andrews and some of his machinists to inspect both craft with us. There may be a few things that will need to be done."

As they left the office, crossing the yard, Captain Jack Benson and Hal Hastings felt exactly as though they were walking on air. Even Hal, quiet as he was, had caught the joy-infection of these orders to proceed to Annapolis. To be sent to the United States Naval Academy on a tour of instruction is what officers of the Navy often call "the prize detail."

Farnum and his two youthful companions went, first of all, to the long, shed-like building in which the third submarine craft to be turned out at this yard was now being built. From inside came the noisy clang of hammers against metal. The ship-builder stepped inside alone, but soon came out, nodding. The three now continued on their way down to the little harbor. All of a sudden the three stopped short, almost with a jerk, in the same second, as though pulled by a string.

At exactly the same instant Jacob Farnum, Captain Jack Benson and Engineer Hal Hastings put up their hands to rub their eyes.

Their senses had told them truly, however. While the "Pollard" rode serenely at her moorings, the "Farnum," the second boat to be launched, was nowhere to be seen!

"What on earth has happened to the other submarine?" gasped the shipbuilder, as soon as he could somewhat control his voice.

What, indeed?

There was not a sign of her. At least, she had not sunk at her moorings, for the buoys floated in their respective places, with no manner of tackle attached to them.

"A submarine boat can't slip its own cables and vanish without human hands!" gasped the staggered Jack Benson.

"There's something uncanny about this," muttered Hal Hastings.

Jacob Farnum stood rooted to the spot, opening and closing his hands in a way that testified plainly to the extent of his bewilderment.

CHAPTER II

HOW EPH FLIRTED WITH SCIENCE

Jack Benson was the first of the trio to move.

Without a word he broke into a run, heading for the narrow little shingle of beach.

"Got an idea, Captain?" shouted Jacob Farnum, darting after his young submarine skipper.

"Yes, sir!" floated back over Jack's shoulder.

"Then what's at the bottom -"

"Eph and the boat, both together, or I miss my guess," Captain Jack shouted back as he halted at the water's edge, where a rowboat lay hauled up on the shore.

Jacob Farnum's face showed suddenly pallid as he, also, reached the beach. Hal, who was in the rear, did not seem so much startled.

"Do you think Eph has gone off on a cruise all alone? - that he has come to any harm?" gasped the shipbuilder.

"I don't know, but I'm not going to worry a mite about Eph Somers until I have to," retorted Jack Benson, easily.

"Eph can generally take care of himself," added Hal Hastings. "He rarely falls into any kind of scrape that he can't climb out of."

"But this is a bad time for him to take the 'Farnum' and cruise away," objected the owner of the yard. "The 'Hudson' may be here at any hour, you know, and we ought to be ready for orders."

As he spoke, Mr. Farnum scanned the horizon away to the south, out over the sea.

"There's a line of smoke, now, and not many miles away," he announced. "It may, as likely as not, be smoke from the 'Hudson's' pipe."

"Going out with us, sir?" inquired Captain Jack Benson, as Hal took his place at a pair of oars.

"Yes," nodded the owner of the yard, dropping into a seat at the stern of the boat, after which Benson pushed off at the bow.

Down on the seashore, on this day just past the middle of October, the air was keen and brisk. There had been frost for several nights past. Sleighing might be looked for in another month.

"Cable's gone from this buoy," declared Captain Jack, as Hal rowed close. "Over to the other one, old fellow."

Here, too, the cable was missing. Evidently the "Farnum" had made a clean get-away. If there had been any accident, it must have taken place after the new submarine boat had slipped away from her moorings.

"Humph!" grunted Jack, scanning the sea. "No sign of the boat anywhere. Eph may be anywhere within twenty miles of here."

"Or within twenty feet, either," grinned Hal, looking down into the waters that were lead-colored under the dull autumn sky.

"What are we going to do, Captain?" inquired Jacob Farnum. "There are Grant Andrews and three of his machinists coming down to the water."

"I reckon, sir, we'd better put them aboard the 'Pollard' first, sir," Benson suggested.

Mr. Farnum nodding, the boat was rowed in to the shore and Andrews and his men were put aboard the "Pollard" at the platform deck. Captain Jack Benson unlocking the door to the conning tower, was himself the first to disappear down below. When he came back he carried a line to which was attached a heavy sounding-lead.

"It won't take us long to sound the deep spots in this little harbor," said the young skipper, as he dropped down once more into the bow of the shore boat. "Row about, Hal, over the places where the submarine could go below out of sight."

As Hal rowed, Skipper Jack industriously used the sounding-lead.

For twenty minutes nothing resulted from this exploration. Then, all of a sudden, Benson shouted:

"Back water, Hal! Easy; rest on your oars. Steady!"

Jack Benson raised the lead two or three feet, then let it down again, playing it up and down very much as a cod fisherman uses his line and hook.

"I'm hitting something, and it is hardly a rock, either," declared young Benson. "Pull around about three points to starboard, Hal, then steal barely forward."

Again Benson played see-saw with his sounding-line over the boat's gunwale.

"If my lead isn't hitting the 'Farnum,'" declared the young skipper, positively, "then it's the 'Farnum's' ghost. Hold steady, now, Hal."

Immediately afterward, Benson caused the lead fairly to dance a jig on whatever it touched at bottom.

"What's the good of that, anyway?" demanded Jacob Farnum.

"You don't think I'm doing this just for fun, do you, sir?" asked Captain Jack, with a smile.

"No; I know you generally have an object when you do anything unusual," responded the shipbuilder, good-humoredly.

"You know, of course, sir, that noises sound with a good deal of exaggeration when you hear them under water?"

"Yes; of course."

"You also know that all three of us have been practicing at telegraphy a good deal during the past few weeks, because every man who follows the sea ought to know how to send and receive wireless messages at need."

"Yes; I know that, Benson."

"Well, sir, I guess that the lead has been hitting the top of the 'Farnum's' hull, and I've been tapping out the signal -"

"The signal, 'Come up - rush!'" broke in Hal, with an odd smile.

"Right-o," nodded Jack Benson.

"How on earth did *you* know what the signal was, Hastings?" demanded Mr. Farnum.

"Why, sir, I've been sitting so that I could see Jack's arm. I've been reading, from the motions of his right arm, the dots and dashes of the Morse telegraph alphabet."

"You youngsters certainly get me, for the things you think of," laughed the shipyard's owner.

"And the 'Farnum,' or whatever it is, is coming up," called Captain Jack, suddenly. "I just felt my lead slide down over the top of her hull. Hard-a-starboard, Hal, and row hard," shouted young Benson, breathlessly.

Though Hastings obeyed immediately he was barely an instant too soon. To his dismay, Mr. Farnum saw something dark, unwieldy, rising through the water. It appeared to be coming up fairly under the stern of the shore boat, threatening to overturn the little craft and plunge them all into the icy water.

Hal shot just out of the danger zone, though. Then a round little tower bobbed up out of the water. Immediately afterward the upper third of a long, cigar-shaped craft came up into view, water rolling from her dripping sides, which glistened brightly as the sun came out briefly from behind a fall cloud.

In the conning tower, through the thick plate glass, the three people in the shore boat made out the carroty-topped head and freckled, good-humored, honest, homely face of Eph Somers. The boat lay on the water, under no headway, drifting slightly with the wind-driven ripples. Then Eph raised the man-hole cover of the top of the conning tower, thrusting out his head to hail them.

"Hey, you landsmen, do you know a buoy from an umbrella?"

"Do *you* know the difference between a Sunday-school text and petty larceny?" retorted Jack Benson, sternly. "What do you mean by taking the submarine without leave?"

"I've been experimenting - flirting with science," responded Eph, loftily. "Say, if you landsmen know a buoy from a banana, get down to the bow moorings of this steel mermaid, and I'll pass you the bow cable. It's a heap easier to lead this submarine horse out of the stall, single-handed, than it is to take him back and tie him."

Hal rowed easily to the buoy, while Eph, returning to the steering wheel and the tower controls, ran the "Farnum," with just bare headway, up to where he could toss the bow cable to those waiting in the boat. A few moments later the stern cable, also, was made fast, in such a way as to allow a moderate swing to the bulky steel craft.

"Now, you can take me ashore, if you feel like it," proposed Eph, standing on the platform deck.

"Not quite yet," returned Skipper Jack, though the small boat lay alongside. "We've got some inspecting to do. But how did you get on board in the first place?"

"Why, the night watchman was in the yard for a few minutes, and I got him to put me on board. I figured I could hail somebody else when I was ready to go on shore."

"But what on earth made you do such a thing?" demanded Captain Jack, in a low tone. "It's really more than you had a right to do, Eph, without getting Mr. Farnum's permission."

"Why, I've known you to take the 'Pollard' and try something when Mr. Farnum wasn't about," retorted Somers, looking surprised.

"You never knew me to do it when I could ask permission, although, as captain, I have the right to handle the boat. But that leave doesn't extend to all the rest, Eph. What were you doing down there, anyway?"

"Why, I came on board, and left the manhole open for ten minutes," answered Somers. "Then I found the cabin thermometer standing at 49 degrees. I wondered how much warmth could be gained by going below the surface. I had been down an hour and five minutes when you began to signal with that sledge-hammer -"

"Sounding-lead," Jack corrected him.

"Well, it sounded like a sledge-hammer, anyway," grinned young Somers. "While I was down below I found that the temperature rose four degrees."

"Part of that was likely due to the warmth of your body, and the heat of the breath you gave off," hinted Benson.

"You could have gotten it up to eighty or ninety degrees by turning on the electric heater far enough," suggested Hal.

"I wanted to see whether it would be warmer in the depths; wanted to find out how low I could go and be able to do without heat in winter," Somers retorted.

"I could have told you that, from my reading, without any experiment," retorted Skipper Jack. "Close your conning tower and go down a little way, and the temperature would gradually rise a few degrees. That's because of the absence of wind and draft. But, if you could go down very, very deep without smashing the boat under the water pressure, you'd find the temperature falling quite a bit."

"Where did you read all that?" inquired Eph, looking both astonished and sheepish.

"Here," replied Jack, going to a small wall book-case, taking down a book and turning several pages before he stopped.

"Just my luck," muttered Eph, disconsolately. "Here I've been dull as ditch-water for an hour, trying to find out something new, and it's all stated in a book printed - ten years ago," he finished, after rapidly consulting the title-page.

Jacob Farnum had been no listener to this conversation. Taking the marine glasses from the conning tower, the shipbuilder was now well forward on the platform deck, scanning what was visible of the steam craft to the southward. At last the yard's owner turned around to say:

"I don't believe you young men can have things ship-shape a second too soon. The craft heading this way has a military mast forward. She must be the 'Hudson.' If there's anything to be done, hustle!"

Jack and Hal sprang below, to scan their respective departments. Five minutes later Grant Andrews hailed from the "Pollard," and Eph rowed over in the shore boat to ferry over the machinists.

Half an hour later Andrews and his men had put in the few needed touches aboard the newer submarine boat. The sun, meanwhile, had gone down, showing the hull of a naval vessel some four miles off the harbor.

Darkness came on quickly, with a clouded sky. As young Benson stepped on deck Grant Andrews followed him.

"All finished here, Grant?" queried the yard's owner.

"Yes, sir. There's mighty little chance to do anything where Hal Hastings has charge of the machinery."

"That's our gunboat out there, I think," went on Mr. Farnum, pointing to where a white masthead light and a red port light were visible, about a mile away.

"Dunhaven must be on the map, all right, if a strange navigating officer knows how to come so straight to the place," laughed Jack Benson.

"Oh, you trust a United States naval officer to find any place he has sailing orders for," returned Jacob Farnum. "I wonder if he'll attempt to come into this harbor?"

"There's safe anchorage, if he wants to do so," replied Captain Jack.

While Somers was busy putting the foreman and the machinists ashore, Mr. Farnum, Jack and Hal remained on the platform deck, watching the approach of the naval vessel, which was now plainly making for Dunhaven.

Suddenly, a broad beam of glaring white light shot over the water, resting across the deck of the "Farnum."

"I guess that fellow knows what he wants to know, now," muttered Benson, blinking after the strong glare had passed.

"There, he has picked up the 'Pollard,' too," announced Hastings. "Now, that commander must feel sure he has sighted the right place."

"There go the signal lights," cried Captain Jack, suddenly. "Hal, hustle below and turn on the electric current for the signaling apparatus."

Then Benson watched as, from the yards high up on the gunboat's signaling mast, colored electric lights glowed forth, twinkling briefly in turn. This is the modern method of signaling by sea at night.

"He wants to know," said Benson, to Mr. Farnum, as he turned, "whether there is safe anchorage for a twelve-hundred-ton gunboat of one hundred and ninety-five feet length."

Reaching the inside of the conning tower at a bound, the young skipper rapidly manipulated his own electric signaling control. There was a low mast on the "Farnum's" platform deck, a mast that could be unstepped almost in an instant when going below surface. So Captain Jack's counter-query beamed out in colors through the night:

"What's your draught?"

"Under present ballast, seventeen-eight," came the answer from the gunboat's signal mast.

"Safe anchorage," Captain Jack signaled back.

"Can you meet us with a pilot?" questioned the on-coming gunboat.

"Yes," Captain Jack responded.

"Do so," came the laconic request.

"That's all, Hal," the young skipper called, through the engine room speaking tube. "Want to row me out and put me aboard the gunboat?"

In another jiffy the two young chums had put off in the boat, Hal at the oars, Jack at the tiller ropes. The gunboat was now lying to, some seven hundred yards off the mouth of the little harbor. Hastings bent lustily to the oars, sending the boat over the rocking water until he was within a hundred yards of the steam craft's bridge.

"Gun boat ahoy!" roared Hal, between his hands. Then, by a slip of the tongue, and wholly innocent of any intentional offense, he bellowed:

"Is that the 'Dad' boat?"

"What's that?" came a sharp retort from the gunboat's bridge. "Don't try to be funny, young man!"

"Beg your pardon, sir. That was a slip of the tongue," Hal replied, meekly, as he colored. "Are you the gunboat 'Hudson?'"

"No; I'm her commanding officer, young man! Who in blazes are you?"

"I'm the goat, it seems," muttered Hastings, under his breath. But, aloud, he replied:

"I have the pilot you requested."

"Then why don't you bring him on board?" came the sharp question. "Did you think I only wanted to look at a pilot?"

"All right, sir. Shall I make fast to your starboard side gangway?" Hal called.

"In a hurry, young man!"

"That's the naval style, I guess," murmured Jack to his chum. "No fooling in the talk. I wonder if that fellow eats pie? Or is his temper due to coffee?"

Answering only with a quiet grin, Hal rowed alongside the starboard side gangway. Jack, waiting, sprang quickly to the steps, ascending, waving his hand to Hal as he went. Young Hastings quickly shoved off, then bent to his oars.

"Where's the pilot?" came a stern voice, from the bridge, as Jack Benson's head showed above the starboard rail.

"I am the pilot, sir," Jack replied.

"Why, you're a boy."

"Guilty," Jack responded.

"What does this fooling mean? You're not old enough to hold a pilot's license."

By this time Benson was on the deck, immediately under the

bridge. A half dozen sailors, forward, were eyeing him curiously.

"I have no license, sir," Jack admitted. "Neither has anyone else at Dunhaven. For that matter, the harbor's a private one, belonging to the shipyard."

"Hasn't Mr. Farnum a *man* he can send out?"

"No one who knows the harbor better than I do, sir."

"Who are you? What are you?"

"Jack Benson, sir. Captain of the Pollard submarine boats."

"Why didn't you tell me that before?"

The question came sharply, almost raspingly.

"Beg your pardon, sir, but you didn't ask me," Jack replied.

"Come up here, Benson," ordered the lieutenant commander, in a loud voice intended to drown out the subdued titter of some of the sailors forward.

Jack ascended to the bridge, to find himself facing a six-footer in his early thirties. There was a younger officer at the far end of the bridge.

"Does Mr. Farnum consider you capable of showing us the way into the harbor?" demanded the commanding officer of the "Hudson."

"I think so, sir. He trusts me with his own boats."

"Then you are -"

"Benson, Mr. Farnum's captain of the submarine boats."

Lieutenant Commander Mayhew gazed in astonishment for a

moment, then held out his hand as he introduced himself, remarking:

"I was told that I would find a very young submarine commander here, but -"

"You didn't expect to find one quite as young," Jack finished, smiling.

"No; I didn't. Mr. Trahern, I want you to know Captain Jack Benson, of the Pollard submarines."

Ensign Trahern also shook hands with young Benson.

"And now," went on the commander of the "Hudson," "I think you may as well show us the way into the harbor."

"You'll want to go at little more than headway, sir," Jack replied. "The harbor is small, though there's enough deep water for you. In parts there are some sand ledges that the tide washes up."

"I can't allow you to pilot us, exactly, but you'll indicate the course to me, won't you, Mr. Benson?"

The "mister" was noticeable, now. Naval officers are chary of their bestowal of the title "captain" upon one who does not hold it in the Army or Navy service.

At Mr. Mayhew's order the "Hudson" was started slowly forward, the searchlight playing about the entrance to the harbor.

"For your best anchorage, sir," declared Captain Jack, after he had brought the gunboat slowly into the harbor, "you will do well to anchor with that main arc-light dead ahead, that shed over there on your starboard beam, and the front end of the submarine shed about four points off your port bow."

Mr. Mayhew slowly manoeuvred his craft, while men stood on the deck below, forward, prepared to heave the bow anchors.

"Go four points over to port, Mr. Trahern," instructed Mr. Mayhew. "Now, back the engines - steady!"

Jack Benson opened his mouth wide. Then, as he saw the way the "Hudson" was backing, he suddenly called:

"Slow speed ahead, quick, sir!"

"You said -" began Mr. Mayhew.

Gr-r-r-r! The stern of the gunboat dug its way into a sand ledge, lifting the stern considerably.

"Slow speed ahead!" rasped Lieutenant Commander Mayhew, sharply.

But the gunboat could not be budged. She was stuck, stern on, fast in the sand-ledge.

"Benson!" uttered the lieutenant commander, bitterly, "I congratulate you. You've succeeded in grounding a United States Naval vessel!"

CHAPTER III

"YOU MAY AS WELL LEAVE THE BRIDGE!"

There was so much of overwhelming censure in the naval officer's tone that Jack's spirit was stung to the quick.

"It's your mistake, sir," he retorted. "You didn't follow the course I advised. You swung the ship around to port, and - "

"Silence, now, if you please, while men are trying to get this vessel out of a scrape a boy got her into," commanded Mr. Mayhem, sternly.

Jack flushed, then bit his tongue. In another moment a pallor had succeeded the red in his face.

He was blamed for the disaster, and he was not really at fault.

Yet, under the rebuke he had just received, he did not feel it his place to retort further for the present.

Mr. Mayhew and Mr. Trahern conferred in low tones for a moment or two.

"You may as well leave the bridge, young man," resumed Mr. Mayhew, turning upon the submarine boy. "You are not likely to be of any use here."

As Jack, burning inwardly with indignation, though managing

to keep outwardly calm, descended to the deck below, he caught sight of Hal Hastings, hovering near in the rowboat. Hal signaled to learn whether he should put in alongside to take off his chum, but Benson shook his head.

Over on the "Farnum" the yard's owner and Eph Somers watched wonderingly. They understood, well enough, that the new, trim-looking gunboat was in trouble, but they did not know that Jack Benson was held at fault.

Down between decks the engines of the "Hudson" were toiling hard to run the craft off out of the sand. Then the machinery stopped. An engineer officer came up from below. He and Mr. Mayhew walked to the stern, while a seaman, accompanying them, heaved the lead, reading the soundings.

"We're stuck good and fast," remarked the engineer officer. "We can't drive off out of that sand for the reason that the propellers are buried in the grit. They'll hardly turn at all, and, when they do, they only churn the sand without driving us off."

"Confound that ignoramus of a boy!" muttered Mr. Mayhew, walking slowly forward. It was no pleasant situation for the lieutenant commander. Having run his vessel ashore, he knew himself likely to be facing a naval board of inquiry.

Hal, finding that the shore boat was not wanted for the present, had rowed over to the "Farnum's" moorings. Now Jacob Farnum came alongside in the shore boat.

"May I speak with your watch officer?" he called.

"I am the commanding officer," Mr. Mayhew called down, in the cold, even, dulled voice of a man in trouble.

"I am Mr. Farnum, owner of the yard. May I come on board?"

"Be glad to have you," Lieutenant Commander Mayhew responded.

So Mr. Farnum went nimbly up over the side.

"May I ask what is the trouble here, sir?" asked the yard's owner.

"The trouble is," replied Mr. Mayhew, "that your enterprising boy pilot has run us aground - hard, tight and fast!"

Jacob Farnum glanced swiftly at his young captain. Jack shook his head briefly in dissent. Jacob Farnum, with full confidence in his young man, at once understood that there was more yet to be learned.

"Come up on the bridge, sir, if you will," requested the commander of the gunboat, who was a man of too good breeding to wish any dispute before the men of the crew. "You may come, too, Benson."

Jack followed the others, including the engineer officer of the "Hudson." Yet Benson was clenching his hands, fighting a desperate battle to get full command over himself. It was hard - worse than hard - to be unjustly accused.

Jacob Farnum wished to keep on the pleasantest terms with these officers of the Navy. At the same time he was man enough to feel determined that Jack, whether right or wrong, should have a full chance to defend himself.

"I understand, sir," began Mr. Farnum, "that you attach some blame in this matter to young Benson?"

"Perhaps he is not to be blamed too much, on account of his extreme youth," responded Mr. Mayhew.

"Forget his youth altogether," urged Mr. Farnum. "Let us treat him as a man. I've always found him one, in judgment, knowledge and loyalty. Do you mind telling me, sir, in what way he erred in bringing you in here?"

"An error in giving his advice," replied Mr. Mayhew. "Or else it was ignorance of how to handle a craft as large as this gunboat. For my anchorage he told me -"

Here the lieutenant commander repeated the first part of Jack's directions correctly, but wound up with:

"He advised me to throw my wheel over four points to port."

"Pardon me, sir," Jack broke in, unable to keep still longer. "What I said, or intended to say, was to bring your vessel so that the forward end of the submarine shed over there would be four points off the port bow."

"What did you hear Mr. Benson say, Mr. Trahern?" demanded the gunboat's commander, turning to the ensign who had stood with him on the bridge.

"Why, sir, I understood the lad to say what he states that he said."

"You are sure of that, Mr. Trahern?"

"Unless my ears tricked me badly," replied the ensign, "Mr. Benson said just what he now states. I wondered, sir, at your calling for slow speed astern."

Lieutenant Commander Mayhew gazed for some moments fixedly at the face of Ensign Trahern. Then, of a sudden, the gunboat's commander, who was both an officer and a gentleman, broke forth, contritely:

"As I think it over, I believe, myself, that Benson advised as he now states he did. It was my own error - I am sure of it now."

Wheeling about, Mayhew held out his right hand.

"Mr. Benson," he said, in a deep voice full of regret, "I was the one in error. I am glad to admit it, even if tardily. Will you pardon my too hasty censure?"

"Gladly, sir," Benson replied, gripping the proffered hand. Jacob Farnum stood back, wagging his head in a satisfied way. It had been difficult for him to believe that his young captain had been at fault in so simple a matter, or in a harbor with which he was so intimately acquainted.

As for the young man himself, the thing that touched him most deeply was the quick, complete and manly acknowledgment of this lieutenant commander.

"Mr. Farnum," inquired the gunboat's commander, "have you any towboats about here that can be used in helping me to get the 'Hudson' off this sand ledge?"

"The only one in near waters, sir," replied the yard's owner, "is a craft, not so very much larger than a launch, that ties up some three miles down the coast. She's the boat I use when I need any towing here. Of course, I have the two torpedo boats, though their engines were not constructed for towing work."

"May I offer a suggestion?" asked Jack, when the talk lagged.

"I'll be glad to have you, Mr. Benson," replied Mr. Mayhew, turning toward the submarine boy.

"Flood tide will be in in about two hours and a half, sir," Benson followed up. "That ought to raise this vessel a good deal. Then, with the towboat Mr. Farnum has mentioned, and with such help as the engines of the submarines may give, together with your own engines, Mr. Mayhew, I think there ought to be a good chance of getting the 'Hudson' afloat with plenty of water under her whole keel. We can even start some of the engines on shore, and rig winches to haul on extra cables. Altogether, we can give you a strong pull, sir."

"That sounds like the best plan to me," nodded Jacob Farnum. "I'll have a message sent at once for that towboat."

A white-coated steward now appeared on deck, moving near the lieutenant commander.

"Is dinner ready, Greers?" called Mr. Mayhew.

"Yes, sir."

"Lay two more plates, then. Mr. Farnum, I trust you and your young submarine commander will sit as my guests to-night."

This invitation the yard's owner accepted, asking only time enough to arrange for keeping some of his workmen over-time, awaiting the coming of flood-tide.

So, presently, Jack and his employer found themselves seated at table in the gunboat's handsome wardroom. Besides the lieutenant commander there were Lieutenant Halpin, two ensigns, two engineer officers and a young medical officer. In the "Hudson's" complement of officers there were also four midshipmen, but these latter ate in their own mess.

The time passed most pleasantly, Mr. Mayhew plainly doing all in his power to atone for his late censure of the submarine boy.

Before dinner was over the small towboat was in the harbor. At the coming of flood tide this towing craft had a hawser made fast to the gunboat. With the help of some of the naval machinists aboard the "Hudson," both submarine craft were also manned and hawsers made fast. Two cables were passed ashore to winches to which power was supplied by the shipyard's engines. When all was ready a mighty pull was given, the gunboat's own propellers taking part in the struggle. For two or three minutes the efforts continued. Then, at last, the "Hudson," uninjured, ran off into deep water and shortly afterwards anchored in safety.

It was a moment of tremendous relief for Mr. Mayhew.

"Call the tugboat captain aboard, and I'll settle with him at my own expense," proposed the lieutenant commander.

"I trust you will think of nothing of the sort," replied Jacob Farnum, quickly. "In this harbor I wish to consider you and your vessel as my guests."

Again Mr. Mayhew expressed his thanks. Presently, glancing ashore through the night, he asked:

"What sort of country is it hereabouts?"

"Mostly flat, as to the surface," Mr. Farnum replied. "If your question goes further, there are some fine roads and several handsome estates within a few miles of here. Mr. Mayhew, won't you and a couple of your officers come on shore with me? I'll telephone for my car and put you over quite a few miles this evening."

"Delighted," replied the commander of the gunboat.

One of the "Hudson's" cutters being now in the water alongside, the party went ashore in this. Jack, after bidding the naval officers good-night, found Hal and Eph, who had just come ashore from supper on board the "Farnum."

"No sailing orders yet, I suppose?" Hal asked.

"None," Jack replied. "I reckon we'll start, all right, some time to-morrow morning."

"What'll we do to-night?" Eph wondered.

"I don't know," replied Jack. "We've few friends around here we need to take the trouble to say good-bye to. We could call on Mrs. Farnum, but I imagine we'd run into the naval party up at the Farnum house. We want to keep a bit in the background with these naval officers, except when they may ask for our company."

"Let's take a walk about the old town, then," Hal suggested.

So the three submarine boys strolled across the shipyard. Just as they were passing through the gate a man of middle height and seemingly about thirty years of age quickened his pace to reach them.

"Is this shipyard open nights?" he queried.

"Only to some employees," Jack answered.

"I suppose Mr. Farnum isn't about?"

"No."

"Captain Benson?"

"Benson is my name."

"This letter is addressed to Mr. Farnum," went on the stranger, "but Mr. Pollard told me I could hand it to you."

Captain Jack took the letter from the unsealed envelope.

"My dear Farnum," ran the enclosure, "since you're short a good machinist for the engine room of the 'Farnum,' the bearer, Samuel Truax, seems to me to be just the man you want. I've examined him, and he understands the sort of machinery we use. Better give him a chance." The note was signed in David Pollard's well-known, scrawly handwriting.

"I'm sorry you can't see Mr. Farnum to-night," said Benson, pleasantly. "He'll be here early in the morning, though."

"When do you sail?" asked Truax, quickly.

"That you would have to ask Mr. Farnum, too," smiled Jack.

"But, see here, Mr. Pollard engaged me to work aboard one of your submarines."

"It looks that way, doesn't it?" laughed the young skipper.

"And you're the captain?"

"Yes; but I can't undertake to handle Mr. Farnum's business for him."

"You'll let me go aboard the craft to sleep for to-night, anyway?" coaxed Truax.

"Why, that's just what I'm not at liberty to do," replied the young submarine captain. "No; I couldn't think of that, in the absence of Mr. Farnum's order."

"But that doesn't seem hardly fair," protested Truax. "See here, I have spent all my money getting here. I haven't even the price of a lodging with me, and this isn't a summer night."

"Why, I'll tell you what I'll do," Benson went on, feeling in one of his pockets. "Here's a dollar. That'll buy you a bed and a breakfast at the hotel up the street. If you want to get aboard with us in time, you'd better show up by eight in the morning."

"But -"

"That's really all I can do," Jack Benson hastily assured the fellow. "I'm not the owner of the boat, and I can't take any liberties. Oh, wait just a moment. I'll see if there's any chance of Mr. Farnum coming back to-night."

Jack knew well enough that there wasn't any chance of Mr. Farnum returning, unless possibly at a very late hour with the naval officers, but the boy had seen the night watchman peering out through the gateway.

Retracing his steps, Jack drew the night watchman inside, whispering:

"Just a pointer for you. You've seen that man on the street with us? He has a letter from Mr. Pollard to Mr. Farnum, but I wouldn't let him in the yard to-night, unless Mr. Farnum appears and gives the order."

"I understand," said the night watchman, nodding.

"That's all, then, and thank you."

Jack Benson hastily rejoined the others on the sidewalk.

"I don't believe, Mr. Truax, it will be worth your while to come here earlier than eight in the morning. Better go to the hotel and tie up to a good sleep. Good night."

"Say, why did you take such a dislike to the fellow?" queried Eph, as the three submarine boys strolled on up the street, Truax following slowly at some distance in the rear.

"I didn't take a dislike to him," Jack replied, opening his eyes wide.

"You choked him off mighty short, then."

"If it looked that way, then I'm sorry," Benson protested, in a tone of genuine regret. "All I wanted to make plain was that I couldn't pass him on to our precious old boat without Mr. Farnum's order."

Truax plodded slowly along behind the submarine boys, a cunning look in the man's eyes as he stared after Jack Benson.

"You're a slick young man, or else a wise one," muttered Truax. "But I think I'm smart enough to take it out of you!"

Nor did Sam Truax go to the hotel. He had his own plans for this evening - plans that boded the submarine boys no good.

The three boys strolled easily about town, getting a hot soda or two, and, finally, drifting into a moving picture show that had opened recently in Dunhaven. This place they did not leave until the show was over. They were half-way home when Captain Jack remembered that he had left behind him a book that he had bought earlier in the evening.

"You fellows keep right on down to the yard. I'll hurry back, get the book and overtake you," he proposed.

Jack ran back, but already the little theatre was closed.

"I'm out that book, then, if we sail in the morning," he muttered, as he trudged along after his friends.

On the way toward the water front Benson had to pass a vacant lot surrounded by a high board fence on a deserted street. He had passed about half way along the length of the fence, when a head appeared over the top followed by a pair of arms holding a small bag of sand. Down dropped the bag, striking Jack Benson on the top of the head, sending him unconscious to the ground.

CHAPTER IV

MR. FARNUM OFFERS ANOTHER GUESS

Close at hand there was a loose board in the fence. Through this Sam Truax thrust his head, peering up and down the street. Not another soul was in sight.

With a chuckle Truax stepped through the hole in the fence. Swiftly he gathered up the young submarine captain, bearing him through the aperture and dropping him on the ground behind the fence. At the same time he took with him the small bag of sand.

"Knocked you out, but I don't believe you'll be unconscious long," mused Truax, standing over his young victim, regarding him critically. "There wasn't steam enough in the blow to hurt you for long. You're sturdy, following the sea all the time, as you do."

With a thoughtful air Sam Truax drew a small bottle from his pocket, sprinkling some of the contents over Jack's uniform coat. Immediately the nauseating smell of liquor rose on the air.

"Now, if someone finds you before you come to, you'll look like a fellow that has been drinking and fighting," muttered Truax under his breath. "If you come to and get back to the yard without help, you'll walk unsteadily and have that smell about your clothes. Usually, it needs only a breath of suspicion to turn folks against a boy!"

Pausing only long enough to learn that Jack's pulses were beating, and that the submarine boy was breathing, Truax stole off into the night, carrying the bag of sand under his overcoat. At one point he paused long enough to empty the sand from the bag over a fence. The bag itself he afterwards burned in the open fireplace in the room assigned to him at Holt's Hotel.

For twenty minutes Jack Benson lay as he had been left. Then he began to stir, and groan. Then he opened his eyes; after a while he managed to sit up.

"Ugh!" he grunted. "What's the odor? Liquor! How does that happen? Oh, my head!"

He got slowly to his feet, using the board fence as a means to help steady himself. Then, though he found himself weak and tormented by the pain in his head, Benson managed to feel his way along the fence until he came to the opening made by the loose board. Holding himself here, he thrust his head beyond.

Now, Hal and Eph, having waited for some time at the shore boat, before going out on board the "Farnum," had at last made up their minds to go back and look for their missing leader. They came along just at the moment that the young captain's head appeared through the opening in the fence.

"There he is," muttered Hal, stopping short. "Gracious! He acts queerly. I wonder if anything can have happened to him? Come along, Eph!"

The two raced across the street.

"Jack, old fellow! What on earth's the matter?" demanded Hal Hastings, anxiously.

"I wish you could tell me," responded Jack Benson, speaking rather thickly, for he was still somewhat dazed. "Oh, my head!"

"There has been some queer work here," muttered Hal in Eph's ear. "Don't torment him with questions. Just help me to get him down to the yard."

While the two submarine boys were guiding their weak, dizzy comrade out to the sidewalk a man came by with a swinging stride. Then he stopped short, staring in amazement.

"Hullo, boys! What on earth has happened?"

It was Grant Andrews, foreman of the submarine work at the yard, and a warm personal friend of Benson's.

"I don't believe the old chap feels like telling us just now," muttered Hal, with a sour face.

"Whiskey!" muttered Andrews, almost under his breath. "What does it mean? Benson never touched a drop of that vile stuff, did he?"

"He'd sooner drown himself," retorted Hal, with spirit.

"Of course he would," agreed Grant Andrews. "But what is the meaning of all this?"

"Oh, there's some queer, hocus-pocus business on foot," muttered Hal, bitterly. "But I don't believe Jack feels much like telling us anything about it at present."

In truth, Jack didn't seem inclined to conversation. He was too sore and dazed to feel like talking. He couldn't collect his ideas clearly. The most that he actually knew was that the pain in his head was tormenting.

"I'll pick him right up in my arms and carry him," proposed Andrews. "I'll take him to Mr. Farnum's office. Then I'll get a doctor. We don't want much noise about this, or folks will be telling all sorts of yarns against Jack Benson and his drinking habits, when the truth is he's about the finest, steadiest young fellow alive!"

Just as Andrews was about to carry his purpose into action, however, an automobile turned the nearest corner and came swiftly toward them. In another instant it stopped alongside. It contained Mr. Farnum and his chauffeur, besides three naval officers.

"What's wrong, Andrews?" called the yard's owner. "Why, that's Jack Benson! What has happened to him?"

Hal and Eph stood supporting their comrade, almost holding him, in fact. Jacob Farnum leaped from his automobile. Lieutenant Commander Mayhew followed him.

"Liquor, eh?" exclaimed the naval officer, the odor reaching his nostrils.

"No such thing," retorted Farnum, turning upon the officer. "At least, Jack Benson has been drinking no such stuff."

"It was only a guess," murmured Mr. Mayhew, apologetically. "You know your young man better than I do, Mr. Farnum."

"There is liquor on his clothing," continued the shipbuilder. "It looks as though someone had assaulted the lad, laid him out, and then sprinkled him. It's a wasted trick, though. I know him too well to be fooled by any such clumsy bit of nonsense."

"A stupid trick, indeed," agreed Lieutenant Commander Mayhew, but the naval officer did not quite share the shipbuilder's confidence in the submarine boy's innocence. Mr. Mayhew had known of too many cases of naval apprentices ruined through weak indulgence in liquor. Indeed, he had even known of rare instances in which cadets had been dismissed from the Naval Academy for the same offense. The lieutenant commander's present doubt of Jack Benson was likely to work to that young man's disadvantage later on.

Others of the party left the auto. Hal and Mr. Farnum got into the tonneau, supporting Jack there between them. Thus they carried him to Mr. Farnum's office at the yard, Grant Andrews then going in the car after a doctor, while the others stretched Jack on the office sofa. The naval officers returned to the "Hudson," at anchor in the little harbor below.

"The young man acts as though he had been struck on the head," was the physician's verdict. "No bones of the skull are broken. The odor of liquor is on his coat, but I can't seem to detect any on the breath."

"Of course you can't," commented Jacob Farnum, crisply. "Will Benson be fit to sail in the morning?"

"I think so," nodded the doctor. "But there ought to be a nurse with him to-night."

"Take my car, Andrews, and get a man nurse at once," directed Mr. Farnum. "Doctor, can the young man be moved to his berth on the 'Farnum'?"

"Safely enough," nodded the medical man. They waited until the nurse arrived, when Jack was put to bed on the newer submarine craft.

Jack slept through the night, moaning once in a while. Mr. Farnum and the Dunhaven doctor were aboard early to look at him. The surgeon from the "Hudson" also came over.

Under the effects of medicine Jack Benson was asleep when, at ten o'clock that morning, the two submarine torpedo boats slipped their moorings, following the "parent boat," the "Hudson," out of the harbor.

Ten minutes later the motion of the sea awoke the young skipper.

CHAPTER V

TRUAX SHOWS THE SULKS

"Hullo!" muttered the young submarine skipper, staring curiously about the little stateroom aft. He had it to himself, the nurse having been put on shore. "Under way, eh? This is the queerest start I ever made on a voyage."

Nor was it many moments later when Jack Benson stood on his feet. His clothes were hung neatly on nails against the wall. One after another Jack secured the garments, slowly donning them.

"How my head throbs and buzzes!" he muttered, his voice sounding unsteady. "Gracious! What could have happened? Let me see. The last I remember - passing that high fence -"

But it was all too great a puzzle. Benson finally decided to stop guessing until some future time. He went on with his dressing. Finally, with his blouse buttoned as exactly as ever, and his cap placed gingerly on his aching head, he opened the stateroom door, stepping out into the cabin.

Accustomed as he was to sea motion, the slight roll of the "Farnum" did not bother the young skipper much. He soon reached the bottom of the short spiral stairway leading up into the conning tower. Up there, in the helmsman's seat, he espied Hal Hastings with his hands employed at the steering apparatus. Hal was looking out over the water, straight ahead.

Victor G. Durham

"Sailing these days without word from your captain, eh?" Jack called, in a voice that carried, though it shook.

"Gracious - you?" ejaculated Hal, looking down for an instant. Then Hastings pressed a button connecting with a bell in the engine room.

"I'm going up there with you," Jack volunteered.

"Right-o, if you insist," clicked Eph Somers, appearing from the engine room and darting to the young skipper's side. True, Jack's head swam a bit dizzily as he climbed the stairs, but Eph's strong support made the task much easier. There was space to spare on the seat beside Hal, and into this Jack Benson sank.

"Say, you ought to sleep until afternoon," was Hastings's next greeting, but Jack was looking out of the conning tower at the scene around him.

The three craft were leaving the coast directly behind. About three hundred yards away, abeam, steamed the "Hudson" at a nine-knot gait.

"The 'Pollard' is on the other side of the gunboat, isn't she?" asked Jack.

"Yes," Hal nodded.

"Naval crew aboard her?"

"Yes; Government has taken full possession of the 'Pollard.'"

"Who's running this boat? Just you and Eph?"

"No; that new man, Truax, is on board, and at the last moment Mr. Farnum put Williamson, one of the machinists, aboard, also. You can send Williamson back from Annapolis whenever you're through with him."

"Williamson is all right," nodded Jack, slowly. "But how about Truax?"

"I think he's going to be a useful man," Hal responded. "He seems familiar with our type of engines. Of course, he knows nothing about the apparatus for submerging the boat or making it dive. But he doesn't need to. Now, Jack, old fellow, we're going along all right. Why not let Eph help you back to your bunk, or one of the seats in the cabin, and have your sleep out?"

"I've had it out," Benson declared, with a laugh. "I'm ready, now, to take my trick at the wheel."

"Nonsense," retorted Hal Hastings. "I've been here a bare quarter of an hour, and I'm good for more work than that. Jack, you're nothing but a fifth wheel. You're not needed; won't be all day, and at night we anchor in some harbor down the coast. Go and rest, like a good fellow."

"Can't rest, when I know I'm doing nothing," Benson retorted, stubbornly. "Besides, this is the first time I've ever found myself moving along in regular formation with the United States Navy. I feel almost as if I were a Navy officer myself, and I mean to make the most of the sensation. Say, Hal, wouldn't it be fine if we really *did* belong to the Navy?"

"Gee-whiz!" murmured young Hastings, his cheeks glowing and his eyes snapping.

"If we only belonged to the old Flag for life, and knew that we were practising on a boat like this as a part of the preparation for real war when it came?"

"*Don't!*" begged Hal, tensely. "For you know, old fellow, it can't come true. Why, we haven't even a residence anywhere, from which a Congressman could appoint one of us to Annapolis!"

Victor G. Durham

"*One* of us?" muttered Jack, scornfully. "Then it would have to be you. *I* wouldn't go, even as a cadet at Annapolis, and leave you behind in just plain, ordinary life, Hal Hastings!"

"Well, it's no use thinking about it," sighed Hal, practically. "Neither one of us is in any danger of getting appointed to Annapolis, so there's no chance that either one of us ever will become an officer in the Navy. Let's not talk about it, Jack. I've been contented enough, so far, but now it makes me almost blue, to think that we can only go on testing and handling submarine craft like these, while others will be their real officers in the Navy, and command them in any war that may come."

Though his head throbbed, and though a dizzy spell came over him every few minutes, Jack Benson stuck it out, up there beside his chum, for an hour. Then, disdaining aid, he crept down the stairs, stretching himself out on one of the cabin seats. Eph brought him a pillow and a blanket. Jack soon slept, tossing uneasily whenever pain throbbed dully in his head.

"Guess I'll go out and have a little look at the young captain," proposed Sam Truax, an hour later.

"Try another guess," retorted Eph, curtly. "You'll stay here in the engine room. Jack Benson isn't going to be bothered in any way."

"I'm not going to bother him; just going to take a look at him," protested Truax, moving toward the door that separated the engine room from the cabin.

But young Somers caught the stranger by the sleeve of the oily jumper that Sam had donned on beginning his work.

"Do you know what folks say about me?" demanded Eph, with a significant glare.

"What do they say?"

"Folks have an idea that, at most times, I'm one of the best-natured fellows on earth," declared Eph, solemnly. "Yet they *do* say that, when I'm crossed in anything my mind's made up to, I can be tarnation ugly. I just told you I don't want the captain disturbed. Do you know, Sam Truax, I feel a queer notion coming over me? I've an idea that that feeling is just plain ugliness coming to life!"

Truax came back from the door, a grin on his face. Yet, when he turned his head away, there was a queer, almost deadly flash in the fellow's eyes.

Jack slept, uneasily, until towards the middle of the afternoon. As soon as Eph found him awake, that young man brought the captain a plate of toast and a bowl of broth, both prepared at the little galley stove.

"Sit up and get away with these," urged Eph, placing the tray on the cabin table. "Wait a minute. I'll prop you up and put a pillow at your back."

"This boat isn't a bad place for a fellow when he's knocked out," smiled Jack.

"Any place ought to be good, where your friends are," came, curtly, from young Somers.

As Captain Jack ate the warm food he felt his strength coming back to him.

"Poor old Hal has been up there in the conning tower all these hours," muttered Captain Jack, uneasily. "He must have that cramped feeling in his hands."

"Humph!" retorted Eph. "Not so you could notice it much, I guess. It's a simpleton's job up in the conning tower to-day. All he has to do is to shift the wheel a little to port, or to starboard, just so as to keep the proper interval from the 'Dad' boat. Besides, I've been up there on relief, for an hour while you slept, and Hal came down and sat with the engines. Cheer up, Jack. No one misses you from the conning tower."

Benson laughed, though he said, warningly:

"I reckon we'll do as well to drop calling the gunboat the 'Dad boat' instead of the 'parent vessel.'"

"Well, you needn't bother at all about the conning tower to-day," wound up Eph, glancing at his watch. "It's after half-past three at this moment and I understand we're to drop anchor about five o'clock."

So Skipper Jack settled back with a comfortable sigh. Truth to tell, it was pleasant not to have any immediate duty, for his head throbbed, every now and then, and he felt dizzy when he tried to walk.

"Who could have hit me in that fashion, last night, and for what earthly purpose?" wondered the boy. "I've had some enemies, in the past, but I don't know a single person about Dunhaven, now who has any reason for wishing me harm."

Never a thought crossed his mind of suspecting Sam Truax. That worthy had come with a note from David Pollard, the inventor of the boats. Sam, therefore, must be all right, the boy reasoned.

Jack lay back on the upholstered seat. He sat with his eyes closed most of the time, though he did not doze. At last, however, he heard the engine room bell sound for reduced speed. Getting up, the young captain made his way to the foot of the conning tower stairs.

"Making port, Hal?" he called.

"Yep," came the reply. "We'll be at anchor in five minutes more."

Jack made his way slowly to the door of the engine room.

"Eph," he called, "as soon as you've shut off speed, take Truax above and you two attend to the mooring."

"Take this other man up with you," urged Sam Truax. "I don't know anything about tying a boat up to moorings."

"Time you learned, then," returned Eph Somers, "if you're to stay aboard a submarine craft."

"Take this other man up with you," again urged Truax.

Eph Somers turned around to face him with a good deal of a glare.

"What ails you, Truax? You heard the captain's order. You'll go with me."

"Don't be too sure of that," uttered Sam Truax, defiantly.

"If you don't go above with me, and if you don't follow every order you get aboard this boat, I know where you *will* go," muttered Eph, decisively.

"Where?" jeered Sam.

"Ashore - in the first boat that can take you there."

"You seem to forget that I'm on board by David Pollard's order," sneered Truax.

"All I am sure of," retorted Eph, "is that Jack Benson is captain on board this craft. That means that he's sole judge of everything here when this boat is cruising. If you were here by the orders of both owners, Jack Benson would fire you ashore for good, just the same, after you've balked at the first order."

"Humph! I -"

Victor G. Durham

Clang! Jangle! The signal bell was sounding.

"Shut up," ordered Eph Somers, briskly. "I've got the engine to run on signal from the watch officer."

There followed a series of signals, first of all for stopping speed, then for a brief reversing of engines. A moment later headway speed ahead was ordered. So on Eph went through the series of orders until the "Farnum" had been manoeuvred to her exact position. Then, from above, Captain Jack's voice was heard, roaring in almost his usual tones:

"Turn out below, there, to help make fast!"

"Take the lever, Williamson," directed Eph. "Come along lively, Truax."

"Humph! Let Williamson go," grumbled Truax.

"You come along with me, my man!" roared Eph, his face blazing angrily. "Hustle, too, or I'll report you to the captain for disobedience of orders. Then you'll go ashore at express speed. Coming?"

Sam Truax appeared to wage a very brief battle within himself. Then, nodding sulkily, he followed.

"Hustle up, there!" Jack shouted down. "We don't want to drift."

Jack Benson stood out on the platform deck, holding to the conning tower at the port side. A naval launch had just placed a buoy over an anchor that had been lowered.

"Get forward, you two," Jack called briskly, "and make the bow cable fast to that buoy."

Hal still sat at the wheel in the tower. As Eph and Truax crept forward over the arched upper hull of the "Farnum," Hal sounded the engine room signals and steered until the boat had gotten close enough to make the bow cable fast. Then the stern cable was made fast, with more line, to another buoy.

"A neat hitch, Mr. Benson," came a voice from the bridge of the "Hudson," which lay a short distance away. Jack, looking up, saw Lieutenant Commander Mayhew leaning over the bridge rail.

"Thank you, sir," Jack acknowledged, saluting the naval officer.

The parent vessel and her two submarine charges now lay at anchor in the harbor at Port Clovis, one of the towns down the coast from Dunhaven. This mooring overnight was to be repeated each day until Annapolis should be reached.

Within fifteen minutes the craft were surrounded by small boats from shore. Some of these contained merchandise that it was hoped sailors would buy. Other boats "ran" for hotels, restaurants, drinking places, amusement halls, and all the varied places on shore that hope to fatten on Jack Tar's money.

"I'd like to go ashore, sir," announced Sam Truax, approaching Captain Jack.

"When?"

"Now."

"For how long?"

"Until ten o'clock to-night."

"Be back by that hour, then," Jack replied. "If you're not, you'll find everything shut tight aboard here."

Truax quickly signaled one of the hovering boats, and put off in it. Eph watched the boat for a few moments before he turned to Captain Jack to mutter:

"Somehow, I wouldn't feel very badly about it if that fellow got lost on shore!"

CHAPTER VI

TWO KINDS OF VOODOO

On the second day of the cruise Jack Benson returned to full duty.

For four nights, in all, the submarine squadron tied up at moorings in harbors along the coast. On the fifth night, as darkness fell, the squadron continued under way, in Chesapeake Bay, for Annapolis was but three hours away.

Immediately after supper Captain Jack took his place in the conning tower. He concerned himself principally with the compass, his only other task being to keep the course by the "Hudson's" lights, for the parent boat supplied in its own conduct all the navigation orders beyond the general course. The "Farnum's" searchlight was not used, the gunboat picking up all the coast-marks as they neared land.

"Annapolis is the place I've always wanted to see," Jack declared, as Hal joined him in the conning tower.

"It's the place where I've always wanted to be a cadet," sighed Hal. "But there's no chance for me, I fear. Jack, I'd rather be an officer of the Navy than a millionaire."

"Same here," replied Jack, steadily. "It's hard to have to feel that I'll never be either."

As she entered the mouth of the Severn River the "Hudson" signaled to the submarines to follow, in file, the "Pollard" leading. A little later the three craft entered the Basin at the Academy. While the gunboat anchored off the Amphitheatre, the two submarine boats were ordered to anchorage just off the Boat House. Then a cutter came alongside.

"The lieutenant commander's compliments to Mr. Benson. Will Mr. Benson go aboard the 'Hudson'?" asked the young officer in command of the cutter. Captain Jack lost no time in presenting himself before the lieutenant commander.

"Mr. Benson," said Mr. Mayhew, after greeting the submarine boy, "your craft will be under a marine guard to-night, and at all times while here at the Naval Academy. If you and your crew would like to spend the night ashore, in the quaint little old town of Annapolis, there's no reason why you shouldn't. But you will all need to report back aboard, ready for duty, by eight in the morning."

Jack thanked the naval commander, then hastened back to the "Farnum" to communicate the news.

"Me for the shore trip," declared Eph, promptly. All the others agreed with him.

"I'll come back by ten o'clock to-night, though," volunteered Sam Truax. "One of the crew ought to be aboard."

"We'll stay ashore," decided Jack, "and return in the morning."

"I'm coming back to-night," retorted Truax.

"Keep still, and follow orders," muttered Eph, digging his elbow into Truax's ribs. "The captain gives the orders here."

Jack, however, had turned away. Within five minutes a boat put off from shore, bringing two soldiers of the marine guard alongside. With them, in the shore boat, was a corporal of the guard.

"Any of your crew coming back to-night, sir?" asked the corporal.

"None," Benson answered. "Will you instruct the sentries to see that none of the crew are allowed aboard during the night?"

"Very good, sir."

The shore boat waited to convey them to the landing. Before going, young Captain Benson closed and locked the manhole entrance to the conning tower. A sullen silence had fallen over Truax. The instructions to the corporal of the guard, and the prompt acceptance of those instructions, told Sam, beyond any doubt, that he was *not* coming back on board that night.

Truax followed the others as they passed through the Academy grounds. Beyond the large, handsome buildings, there was not much to be seen at night. Lights shone behind all the windows in Cadet Barracks. Nearly all of the cadets of the United States Navy were in their quarters, hard at study. Here and there a marine sentry paced. A few naval officers, in uniform, passed along the walks. That was all, and the submarine party had crossed the grounds to the gate through which they were to pass into the town of Annapolis.

"Coming with us, Truax?" asked Williamson, as the party passed out into a dimly lighted street.

"No," replied the fellow, sullenly. "I'll travel by myself."

"You're welcome to," muttered Eph, under his breath.

The others climbed the steps to the State Capitol grounds, continuing until they reached one of the principal streets of the little town.

"Say, but this place must have gone to sleep before we got ashore," grumbled Eph. "Hanged if I don't think Dunhaven is a livelier little place!"

"There isn't much to do, except to wander about a bit, then go to the Maryland House for a good sleep on shore," Jack admitted.

For more than an hour the submarine boys wandered about. The principal streets contained some stores that had a bright, up-to-date look, and in these principal streets the evening crowds much resembled those to be found in any small town. There were other streets, however, on which there was little traffic. In some of these quieter streets were quaint, old-fashioned houses built in the Colonial days.

"Annapolis is more of a place to see by daylight, I reckon," suggested Hal. "How about that sleep, Jack?"

"The greatest fun, by night, I guess, consists in finding a drug-store and spending some of our loose change on ice cream sodas," laughed the young submarine skipper.

This done, they found their way to the Maryland House. Jack and Hal engaged a room together, Eph and Williamson taking the adjoining one.

"As for me, in an exciting place like this," grimaced Eph, "I'm off for bed."

Williamson followed him upstairs. For some minutes Hal sat with his chum in the hotel office. Then Jack went over and talked with the night clerk for a few moments.

"There's a place near here, Hal, where a fellow can get an oyster fry," Benson explained, returning to his chum. "With that information came the discovery that I have an appetite. Come and join me?"

"No," gaped Hal. "I reckon I'll go up and turn in."

"I'll be along in half an hour, then."

Jack found the oyster house readily. As he entered the little, not over-clean place, he found himself the only customer. He gave his order, then picked up the local daily paper. As he ate, Jack found himself yawning. The drowsiness of Annapolis by night was coming upon him. Little did he dream how soon he was to discover that Annapolis, in some of its parts, can be lively enough.

As he paid his bill and stepped to the street, a young mulatto hurried up to him.

"Am Ah correct, sah, in supposin' yo' Cap'n Jack Benson?"

"That's my name," Jack admitted.

"Den Ah's jes' been 'roun' to de hotel, lookin' fo' yo', sah. One ob yo' men, Mistah Sam Truax, am done took sick, an' he done sent me fo' yo'."

"Truax ill? Why, I saw him a couple of hours ago, and he looked as healthy as a man could look," Jack replied, in astonishment.

"I reckon, sah, he's mighty po'ly now, sah," replied the mulatto. "He done gib me money fo' to hiah a cab an' take yo' to him. Will yo' please to come, sah?"

"Yes," agreed Jack. "Lead the way."

"T'ank yo', sah; t'ank yo', sah. Follow me, sah."

Jack's mulatto guide led him down the street a little way, then around a corner. Here a rickety old cab with a single horse attached, waited. A gray old darkey sat on the driver's seat.

"Step right inside, sah. We'll be dere direckly. Marse Truax'll be powahful glad to see yo', sah."

"See here," demanded Jack, after they had driven several blocks at a good speed, "Truax hasn't been getting into any drinking scrapes, has he? Hasn't been getting himself arrested, has he?"

For young Benson had learned, from the night clerk at the hotel, that, quiet and "dead" as Annapolis appears to the stranger, there are "tough" places into which a seafaring stranger may find his way.

"No, sah; no, sah," protested the mulatto. "Marse Truax done got sick right and proper."

"Why, confound it, we're leaving the town behind," cried Jack, a few moments later, after peering out through the cab window.

"Dat's all right, sah. Dere ain' nuffin' to be 'fraid ob, sah."

"Afraid?" uttered Jack, scornfully, with a side glance at the mulatto. The submarine boy felt confident that, in a stretch of trouble, he could thrash this guide of his in very short order.

"Ah might jess well tell yo' wheah we am gwine, sah," volunteered the mulatto, presently.

"Yes," Benson retorted, drily. "I think you may."

"Marse Truax, sah, he done hab er powah ob trouble, sah, las' wintah, wid rheumatiz, sah. He 'fraid he gwine cotch it again dis wintah, sah. Now, sah, dere am some good voodoo doctahs 'roun' Annapolis, so Marse Truax, he done gwine to see, sah, what er voodoo can promise him fo' his rheumatiz. I'se a runnah, sah, for de smahtest ole voodoo doctah, sah, in de whole state ob Maryland."

"Then you took Truax to a voodoo doctor to-night?"

demanded Jack, almost contemptuously.

"Yes, sah; yes, sah."

"I thought Truax had more sense than to go in for such tomfoolery," Jack Benson retorted, bluntly.

The mulatto launched into a prompt, energetic defense of the voodoo doctors. Young Benson had heard a good deal about these clever old colored frauds. In spite of his contempt, the submarine boy found himself interested. He had heard about the charms, spells, incantations and other humbugs practised on colored dupes and on some credulous whites by these greatest of all quacks. The voodoo methods of "healing" are brought out of the deepest jungles of darkest Africa, yet there are many ignorant people, even among the whites, who believe steadfastly in the "cures" wrought by the voodoo.

While the mulatto guide was talking, or answering Jack's half-amused questions, the cab left Annapolis further and further behind.

"Yo' see, sah," the guide went on, "Marse Truax wa'n't in no fit condition, sah, to try de strongest voodoo medicine dat he called fo'. So, w'ile de voodoo was sayin' his strongest chahms, Marse Truax done fall down, frothin' at de mouth. He am some bettah, now, sah, but he kain't be move' from de voodoo's house 'cept by a frien'."

"I'll get a chance to see one of these old voodoo frauds, anyway," Jack told himself. "This new experience will be worth the time it keeps me out of my bed. What a pity Hal missed a queer old treat like this!"

When the cab at last stopped, Benson looked out to find that the place was well down a lonely country road, well lined with trees on either side. The house, utterly dark from the outside, was a ramshackle, roomy old affair.

"Shall Ah wait fo' yo'?" asked the old colored driver.

"Yes, wait for me," directed Jack, briefly.

"Yeah; wait fo' de gemmun. He's all right," volunteered the mulatto.

"Mebbe yo' kin see some voodoo wo'k, too, ef yo's int'rested," hinted the guide, in a whisper, as he fitted a key to a lock, and swung a door open. In a hallway stood a lighted lantern, which the guide picked up.

"Now, go quiet-lak, on tip-toe. Sh!" cautioned the guide, himself moving stealthily into the nearest room. Jack Benson began to feel secretly awestruck and "creepy," though he was too full of grit to betray the fact.

At the further end of the room the guide, holding the lantern behind his body as though by accident, threw open another door.

"Pass right on through dis room, ahead ob me, sah," begged the guide, respectfully.

But Jack drew back, instinctively, out of the darkness.

"Don' yo', a w'ite man, be 'fraid ob ole voodoo house," advised the mulatto, still speaking respectfully.

Afraid? Of course not. Relying on his muscle and his agility, Jack stepped ahead. By a sudden jerk of his arm the mulatto guide shook out the flame in the lantern.

"Here, you! What are you about?" growled Jack Benson, wheeling like a flash upon his escort.

"Go 'long, yo' w'ite trash!" jeered the mulatto. He gave the boy a sudden, forceful shove.

Jack Benson, under the impetus of that push, staggered ahead, seeking to recover his balance. Without a doubt he would have done so, but, just then, the floor under his feet ended. With a yell of dismay, the submarine boy tottered, then plunged down, alighting on a bed of soft dirt many feet below.

CHAPTER VII

JACK FINDS SOMETHING "NEW," ALL RIGHT

Jack Benson was on his feet in an instant. An angrier boy it would have been hard to find.

From overhead came the sound of a loud guffaw.

"Oh, you infernal scoundrel!" raged the submarine boy, shaking his fist in the dark.

"W'at am de matter wid yo', w'ite trash?" came the jeering query.

"Let me get my hands on you, and I'll show you!" quivered Benson.

"Yah! Listen to yo'! Yo' wait er minute, an' Ah'll show yo' a light."

Gr-r-r-r! Gr-r-r-r! That sound from overhead was not pleasant. Jack, in the few seconds that were left to him, could only guess as to the cause of the sounds. Then, some fifteen feet over his head, a tiny flame sputtered. This match-end was carried to the wick of the lantern that the yellowish guide had been carrying, and now the light illumined the place into which Jack Benson had fallen.

That place was a square-shaped pit, with boarded sides. Up

above, on a shelf of flooring, knelt the late guide, grinning down with a look of infernal glee. On either side of the mulatto stood a heavy-jowled bull-dog. Both brutes peered down, showing their teeth in a way to make a timid man's blood run cold.

"Put those dogs back and come down here," challenged Jack, shaking his fist. "Come down, and I'll teach you a few things, you rascal!"

"Don' yo' shake yo' fist at me, or dem dawgs will sure jump down and tackle yo'," grinned the guide, gripping at the collars of the brutes, which, truly, showed signs of intending to spring below.

Jack fell back, his hands dropping to his sides. Had there been but one dog, the submarine boy, with all his grit forced to the surface, might have chosen to face the brute, hoping to despatch it with a well-aimed kick. But with two dogs, both intent on "getting" him, young Benson knew that he would stand the fabled chance of a snow-flake on a red-hot stove.

"Dat's right, gemmun, yo' keep cool," observed the mulatto, mockingly.

"You've decoyed me - trapped me here with a mess of lies," flung back Captain Jack, angrily. "What's your game?"

"Dis am a free lodgin' house - ho, ho, ho!" chuckled the late guide. "Ah's gwine gib yo' er place to sleep fo' de night. Yo' sho'ly must feel 'bleeged to me - ho, ho, ho!"

"You lied to me about Sam Truax!"

"Yeah! Ah done foun' dat was de name ob a gemmun in yo' pahty dat wasn't wid yo'. Truax do as well as any odder name - yah! Now, Ah's gwine leab yo' heah t' git a sleep. Ah'll toss down some blankets. 'Pose yo'se'f and gwine ter sleep, honey. Don't try to clim' up outer dat, or dem dawgs'll sho'ly jump down at yo'. Keep quiet, an' go ter sleep, an' de dawgs done lay heah an' jest watch. But don' try nuffin' funny, or de dawgs'll sho'ly bring trubble to yo'. Dem is trained dawgs - train' fo' dis business ob mine. Ho, ho, ho!"

Mulatto and light vanished, but enraged, baffled, helpless Captain Jack could hear the two dogs moving about ere they settled down on the shelf of flooring overhead.

"No matter how much of a liar that rascal is, he didn't lie to me about the dogs," reflected Jack, his temper cooling, but his bitterness increasing. "They're fighting dogs, and one wrong move would bring them bounding down here on me - the two together. Ugh-gh!"

After a few moments the mulatto reappeared with a light and tossed down three heavy blankets.

"Now, Ah's gwine leave yo' fo' de night," clacked the late guide. "Ef yo' done feel lonesome, yo' jes' whistle de dawgs down to yo'. Dey'll come!"

While the light was still there Benson, in raging silence, gathered the blankets and arranged them.

"Roll up one fo' a pillow, under yo' haid," grinned the mulatto. "Dat's all right, sah. Now, good night, Marse Benson. Ef yo' feel lonesome, Marse Benson, jes' whistle fo' de dawgs. *Dey'll come!*"

The light vanished while the mulatto's sinister words were ringing in the boy's ears. Would the dogs jump down? Jack knew they would, at the first false move or sound on his part. He huddled softly, stealthily, on the blankets, there in the darkness.

As he lay there, thinking, Benson's sense of admiration gradually got to the surface.

"Well, of all the slick man-traps!" he gasped. "I never heard of anything more clever. Nor was there ever a bigger idiot than I, to walk stupidly into this same trap! What's the game, I wonder? Robbery, it must be. And I have a watch, some other little valuables and nearly a hundred and fifty dollars in money on me. Oh, I'm the sleek, fat goose for plucking!"

Lying there, in enforced stillness, Jack Benson, after an hour or so, actually fell asleep. A good, healthy sleeper at all times, he slumbered on through the night. Once he awoke, just a trifle chilled. He heard one of the dogs snoring overhead. Crawling under one of the blankets, Benson went to sleep again.

"Hey, yo', Marse Benson. It am mawnin'. Time yo' was wakin' up an' movin' erlong!"

It was the voice of the same mulatto, calling down into the pit. Again the rays of the lantern illumined the darkness. Both bull-dogs displayed their ferocious muzzles over the edge of the pit. Jack sat up cautiously, not caring to attract unfriendly interest from the dogs.

"Ah want yo' to take off all yo' clothes 'cept yo' undahclothes, an' den Ah'll let down a string fo' yo' to tie 'em to," declared the mulatto, grinning. "Yo' needn't try ter slip yo' wallet, nor nuffin' outer mah sight, cause Ah'll be watchin'. Now, git a hurry on, Marse Benson, or Ah'll done push dem dawgs ober de aidge ob dis flooring."

Jack hesitated only a moment. Then, with a grunt of rage, he began removing his outer garments. Down came a twine, to the lower end of which the boy made fast his garments, one after another. His money and valuables went up in the pockets, for the sharp eyes of the mulatto could not have been eluded by any amateur slight-of-hand.

"Now, yo' cap an' yo' shoes," directed the grinning monster above.

Victor G. Durham

These, too, Benson passed up at the end of the cord. The mulatto disappeared, leaving the two dogs still on guard. At last, back came the light and the yellowish man with it.

"Yo' sho' is good picking, Marse Benson," grinned the guide of the night before. "Yo' has good pin feathers. Ah hope Ah'll suttinly meet yo' again."

"I hope we do meet at another time!" Jack Benson flared back, wrathily. The cool insolence of the fellow cut him to the marrow, yet where was the use of disobeying a rascal flanked by two such willing and capable dogs?

"Now, yo' jes' put dese t'ings on, Marse Benson, ef yo' please, sah," mocked the mulatto, tossing down some woefully tattered, nondescript garments, and, after them, a battered, rimless Derby hat and a pair of brogans out at the toes.

"I'll be hanged if I'll put on such duds!" quivered Jack.

"Jes' as yo' please, ob co'se, Marse Benson," came the answer, from above. "But, ef yo' don' put dem t'ings on, yo'll sho'ly hab ter gwine back ter 'Napolis in yo' undahclo's. An' yo's gwine back right away, too, so, ef yo' wants ter gwine back weahin' ernuff clo'es -"

"Oh, well, then -!" ground out the submarine boy, savagely enough.

He attired himself in these tattered ends of raiment. Had he not been so angry he must have roared at sight of his comical self when the dressing was completed.

CHAPTER VIII

A YOUNG CAPTAIN IN TATTERS

"Now, yo'll do, Ah reckons."

With that, the mulatto guide of the night before threw down one end of an inch rope.

"Ah reckon yo's sailor ernuff to clim' dat. Come right erlong, 'less yo' wants de dawgs ter jump down dar."

"But they'll tackle me if I come up," objected Jack Benson.

"No, dey won't. Dem dawgs is train' to dis wo'k. Ah done tole yo' dat. Come right erlong. Ah'll keep my two eyes on dem dawgs."

It looked like a highly risky bit of business, but Jack told himself that, now he had been deprived of his valuables, this yellow worthy must be genuinely anxious to be rid of the victim. So he took hold of the rope and began to climb. The mulatto and the dogs disappeared from the upper edge of the pit.

As his head came up above the level of the flooring Benson saw the mulatto and the dogs in the next room, the connecting door of which had been taken from its hinges.

"Come right in, Marse Benson. Dere ain' nuffin' gwineter hu't yo'," came the rascal's voice reassuringly. Jack obeyed by stepping into the next room, though he kept watch over the dogs out of the corners of his eyes.

"Now, yo' lie right down on de flo', Marse Benson," commanded the master of the situation. "Ah's gotter tie yo' up, befo' Ah can staht yo' back ter 'Napolis, but dere ain' no hahm gwine come ter yo'."

Making a virtue of necessity, Captain Jack lay down as directed, passing his hands behind his back. These were deftly secured, after which his ankles were treated in the same fashion. Immediately the mulatto, who was strong and wiry, lifted the boy and the lantern together. The dogs remaining behind, Jack was carried out into the yard, where he discovered that daylight was coming on in the East. He was dumped on the ground long enough to permit his captor to lock the door securely. Then the submarine boy was lifted once more, carried around the corner of the house and dumped in the bottom of a shabby old delivery wagon. A canvas was pulled over him, concealing him from any chance passer. Then the mulatto ran around to the seat, picking up the reins and starting the horse.

It seemed like a long drive to the boy, though Benson was certainly in no position to judge time accurately. At last the team was halted, along a stretch of road in a deep woods. The mulatto lifted the submarine boy out to the ground.

"Now, w'en yo's got yo' se'f free, yo' can take de road in dat direckshun," declared the fellow, pointing. "Bimeby yo' come in sight ob de town. Now, Marse Benson, w'at happen to yo' las' night am all in de co'se ob a lifetime, an' Ah hope you ain't got no bad feelin's. Yo' suttinly done learn somet'ing new in de way ob tricks. Good-bye, sah, an' mah compliments to yo', Marse Benson."

With that the guide of the night before swiftly cut the cords at Jack's wrists, then as swiftly leaped to the seat of the wagon, whipping up the horse and disappearing in a cloud of dust.

Jack, having now no knife, and the bonds about his ankles being tied with many hard knots, spent some precious minutes in freeing his feet. At last he stood up, fire in his eyes.

"Oh, pshaw! There's no sense in trying to run after that rascal and his wagon," decided the young submarine skipper. "I haven't the slightest idea what direction he took after he got out of sight, and - oh, gracious! I'm under orders to be aboard the 'Farnum' at eight this morning. And on Mr. Farnum's business, at that!"

Clenching his hands vengefully, Jack started along in the direction pointed out by his late captor. Brisk walking wore some of the edge off his great wrath. Catching a comprehensive glimpse of himself, Jack could not keep back a grim laugh.

"Well, I certainly am a dandy to spring myself on the trim and slick Naval Academy!" he gritted. "What a treat I'll be to the cadets! That is, if the sentry ever lets me through the gate into the Academy grounds."

As he hurried along, Jack Benson decided that he simply could not go to the Naval Academy presenting any such grotesque picture as he did now. Yet he had no money about him with which to purchase more presentable clothes in town. So he formed another plan.

Within a few minutes he came in sight of Annapolis. Hurrying on faster, he at last entered the town. The further he went the more painfully conscious the boy became of the ludicrous appearance that he made. He saw men and women turn their heads to look after him, and his cheeks burned to a deep scarlet that glowed over the sea-bronze of his skin.

"The single consolation I have is that not a solitary person in town knows me, anyway," he muttered. Then he caught sight of a clock on a church steeple - twenty-five minutes of eight.

Victor G. Durham

"That means a fearful hustle," he muttered, and went ahead under such steam that he all but panted. At last he came to the Maryland House, opposite the State Capitol grounds. Into the office of the hotel he darted, going straight up to the desk.

A clerk who had been on duty for hours, and who was growing more drowsy every moment, stared at the boy in amazement.

"See here, you ragamuffin, what -"

"My name is Benson," began the boy, breathlessly. "I'm a guest of the house - arrived last night. I -"

"You, a guest of *this* house?" demanded the clerk of the most select hotel in the town. "You -"

That was as far as the disgust of the clerk would permit him to go in words. A score of well-dressed gentlemen were staring in astonishment at the scene. The clerk nodded to two stout porters who had suspended their work nearby.

It had been Jack Benson's purpose to go to his room and keep out of sight, while despatching one of the colored bell-boys of the hotel with a note to Hal Hastings, asking that chum to send him up a uniform and other articles of attire. However, before the young submarine captain fully realized what was happening, the two porters had seized him. Firmly, even though gently, they hustled him out through the entrance onto the street.

"Scat!" advised one of the pair.

Jack started to protest, then realized the hopelessness of such a course. In truth, he did not blame the hotel folks in the least.

"Oh, well," he sighed, paling as soon as the new flush of mortification had died out, "there's nothing for it but to hurry to the Academy. I hope the sentries won't shoot when they see me," he added, bitterly.

Across the State Capitol grounds he hurried, then down through a side street until he arrived at the gate of the Academy grounds.

"Halt!" challenged a sentry, as soon as Jack showed his face through the gateway.

Young Benson stopped, bringing his heels together with a click.

"What do you want? Where are you going?" demanded the marine.

"I know I look pretty tough," Jack admitted, shamefacedly. "But I belong aboard the 'Farnum,' one of the submarines that arrived last night. And I'm due there at this minute. Please don't delay me."

"All right," replied the sentry, after surveying the boy from head to foot once more. Then he added, in a lower tone, with just the suspicion of a grin showing at the corners of his mouth:

"Say, friend, for a stranger, you must have had a high old frolic in the town last night."

Jack frowned. The sentry's grin broadened a bit. As he did not offer to detain the boy longer, Benson hurried on along one of the walks. He took as short a course as he could making straight for the Basin, where he made out the "Hudson" and the two submarines.

"Hey! There's the captain!" shouted Eph, wonderingly, for Somers's eyes were sharp at all times.

Out of the conning tower sprang Hal Hastings, looking eagerly in the direction in which Eph Somers pointed:

"Eh?" muttered another person, lounging near the rail of the gunboat. Then Lieutenant Commander Mayhew, after a keen, wholly disapproving look at the hard-looking figure of a young man at the landing, started, as he muttered:

"Benson, by all that's horrible! How did he come to be in that fearful shape? He must have been in one of the worst resorts within miles of Annapolis!"

"This isn't the first time the young man has come back the worse for wear," the lieutenant commander continued, under his breath. "His friends were loyal enough to him, that time. I wonder if they can be, to-day?"

One of the shore boats, waiting about in the Basin, put young Benson aboard the "Farnum" as soon as he explained who he was. Hal and Eph stood awaiting the coming of their young commander, their faces full of concern and anxiety. Both gripped Jack's hand as soon as he gained the platform deck of the submarine.

"Come below," whispered Hal. "We'll talk there. You need a bath and to get into a uniform as quickly as you can."

This need Jack Benson proceeded to realize without an instant's delay. While he washed himself off, in one of the staterooms aft, he talked through the door, which had been left ajar. He continued his story while he dressed.

"We were fearfully anxious this morning," Hal confessed. "I went to sleep last night, and didn't know of your absence until this morning. Then Eph and I decided to come on down to the boat to see if you were here. We were just planning to send quiet word to the Annapolis police when Eph spotted you coming."

"And Truax?" inquired Captain Jack.

"He and Williamson are forward in the engine-room, now, at breakfast."

"Oh, well, Truax wouldn't know anything about the scrape, anyway," returned Jack. "His name was learned and used - that's all."

"Are you going to try to find that place, catch the mulatto and force the return of your money?" demanded Eph Somers.

"I've got to think that over," muttered Jack, as he drew on a spick-and-span uniform blouse. "I don't know whether there'll be any use in trying to find that mulatto. I haven't the least idea where his place is. Even if I found it, it's ten to one I wouldn't find the fellow there."

"'Farnum,' ahoy!" roared a voice alongside, the voice coming down through the open conning tower.

Eph ran to answer. When he returned, he announced:

"Compliments of Lieutenant Commander Mayhew, and will Mr. Benson wait on the lieutenant commander on board the parent boat?"

"I will," assented Jack, with a wry face, "and here's where I have to do some tall but truthful explaining to a man who isn't in the least likely to believe a word I say. I can guess what Mr. Mayhew is thinking, and is going to keep on thinking!"

CHAPTER IX

TRUAX GIVES A HINT

It was a tailor-made, clean, crisp and new-looking young submarine commander who stepped into the naval cutter alongside.

Jack Benson looked as natty as a young man could look, and his uniform was that of a naval officer, save for the absence of the insignia of rank.

Up the side gangway of the gunboat Jack mounted, carrying himself in the best naval style. On deck stood a sentry, an orderly waiting beside him.

"Lieutenant Commander Mayhew will see you in his cabin, sir," announced the orderly. "I will show you the way, sir."

Mr. Mayhew was seated before a desk in his cabin when the orderly piloted the submarine boy in. The naval officer did not rise, nor did he ask the boy to take a seat. Jack Benson was very well aware that he stood in Mr. Mayhew's presence in the light of a culprit.

"Mr. Benson," began Mr. Mayhew, eyeing him closely, "you are not in the naval service, and are not therefore amenable to its discipline. At the same time, however, your employers have furnished you to act, in some respects, as a civilian instructor in submarine boating before the cadets. While you are here on that duty it is to be expected, therefore, that you will conform generally to the rules of conduct as laid down at the Naval Academy."

"Yes, sir," replied Jack.

"As I am at present in charge of the submarine purchased by the United States from your company, and at least in nominal charge of the 'Farnum,' as well, I am, in a measure, to be looked upon, for the present, as your commanding officer."

"Yes, sir," assented the boy.

"You came aboard your craft, this morning, in a very questionable looking condition."

"Yes, sir."

Jack Benson's composure was perfect. His sense of discipline was also exact. He did not propose to offer any explanations until such were asked of him.

"Have you anything to say, Mr. Benson, as to that condition, and how you came to be in it?"

"Shall I explain it to you, sir?"

"I shall be glad to hear your explanation."

Thereupon, the submarine boy plunged into a concise description of what had happened to him the night before. The lieutenant commander did not once interrupt him, but, when Jack had finished, Mr. Mayhew observed:

"That is a very remarkable story, Mr. Benson. Most remarkable."

"Yes, sir, it is. May I ask if you doubt my story?"

Jack looked straight into the officer's eyes as he put the question bluntly. An officer of the Army or of the Navy *must not* answer a question untruthfully. Neither, as a rule, may he make an evasive answer. So the lieutenant commander thought a moment, before he replied:

"I don't feel that I know you well enough, Mr. Benson, to express an opinion that might be wholly fair to you. The most I can say, now, is that I very sincerely hope such a thing will not happen again during your stay at the Naval Academy."

"It won't, sir," promised Jack Benson, "if I have hereafter the amount of good judgment that I ought to be expected to possess."

"I hope not, Mr. Benson, for it would destroy your usefulness here. A civilian instructor here, as much as a naval instructor, must possess the whole confidence and respect of the cadet battalion. I hope none of the cadets who may have seen you this morning recognized you."

Then, taking on a different tone, Mr. Mayhew informed his young listener that a section of cadets would board the "Farnum" at eleven that morning, another section at three in the afternoon, and a third at four o'clock.

"Of course you will have everything aboard your craft wholly shipshape, Mr. Benson, and I trust I hardly need add that, in the Navy, we are punctual to the minute."

"You will find me punctual to the minute before, sir."

"Very good, Mr. Benson. That is all. You may go."

Jack saluted, then turned away, finding his way to the deck. The cutter was still alongside, and conveyed him back to the "Farnum."

"Mr. Mayhew demanded your story, of course?" propounded

Hal Hastings. "What did he think?"

"He didn't say so," replied Jack Benson, with a wry smile, "but he let me see that he thought I was out of my element on a submarine boat."

"How so?"

"Why, it is very plain that Mr. Mayhew thinks I ought to employ my time writing improbable fiction."

"Oh, Mayhew be bothered!" exploded Eph.

"Hardly," retorted Jack. "Mr. Mayhew is an officer and a gentleman. I admit that my yarn *does* sound fishy to a stranger. Besides, fellows, Mr. Mayhew represents the naval officers through whose good opinion our employers hope to sell a big fleet of submarine torpedo boats to the United States Government."

"Then what are you going to do about it?" asked Hal, as the three boys reached the cabin below.

"First of all, I'm going to rummage about and get myself some breakfast."

"If you do, there'll be a fight," growled Eph Somers. "I'll hash up a breakfast for you."

"And, afterwards?" persisted Hal.

"I'm going to try to win Mr. Mayhew's good opinion, and that of every other naval officer or cadet I may happen to meet."

"Why the cadets, particularly?" asked Eph Somers.

"Because, for one business reason, the cadets are going to be the naval officers of to-morrow, and the Pollard Submarine Boat Company hopes to be building craft for the Navy for a good many years to come."

"Good enough!" nodded Hal, while Eph dodged away to get that breakfast ready.

Sam Truax lounged back in the engine room, smoking a short pipe. With him stuck Williamson, for Eph had privately instructed the machinist from the Farnum yard not to leave the stranger alone in the engine room.

"Why don't you go up on deck and get a few whiffs of fresh air?" asked Truax.

"Oh, I'm comfortable down here," grunted the machinist, who was stretched out on one of the leather-cushioned seats that ran along the side of the engine room.

"I should think you'd want to get out of here once in a while, though," returned Truax.

"Why?" asked the machinist. "Anything you want to be left alone here for?"

"Oh, of course not," drawled Truax, blowing out a cloud of tobacco smoke.

"Then I guess I'll stay where I am," nodded Williamson.

"Sorry, but you'll have to stop all smoking in here now," announced Eph, thrusting his head in at the doorway. "There'll be a lot of cadets aboard at eleven o'clock, and we want the air clear and sweet. You'd better go all over the machinery and see that everything is in applepie order and appearance. Mr. Hastings will be in here soon to inspect it."

"Just what rank does *that* young turkey-cock hold on board?" sneered Truax, when the door had closed.

"Don't know, I'm sure," replied Williamson. "All I know is

that the three youngsters are aboard here to run the boat and show it off to the best advantage. My pay is running right along, and I've no kick at taking orders from any one of them."

"This is where I go on smoking, anyway," declared Truax, insolently, striking a match and lighting his pipe again. Williamson reached over, snatching the pipe from between the other man's teeth and dumping out the coals, after which the machinist coolly dropped the pipe into one of his own pockets.

"If you go on this way," warned Williamson, "Captain Benson will get it into his head to put you on shore in a jiffy, and for good."

"I'd like to see him try it," sneered Sam Truax.

"You'll get your wish, if you go on the way you've been going!"

"Humph! I don't believe the Benson boy carries the size or the weight to put me ashore."

"He doesn't need any size or weight," retorted Williamson, crisply. "If Captain Benson wants you off this boat, it's only the matter of a moment for him to get a squad of marines on board - and you'll march off to the 'Rogues' March.'"

"So that's the way he'd work it, eh?" demanded Sam Truax, turning green and ugly around the lips.

"You bet it is," retorted the machinist. "We're practically a part of the United States Navy for these few days, and naval rules will govern any game we may get into."

On that hint things went along better in the engine room. When Hal Hastings came in to inspect he found nothing to criticise.

At the minute of eleven o'clock a squad of some twenty cadets

Victor G. Durham

came marching down to the landing in front of the boat house. There Lieutenant Commander Mayhew and one of his engineer officers met them. Two cutters manned by sailors brought the party out alongside, where Jack and Hal stood ready to receive them.

A very natty looking squad of future admirals came aboard, grouping themselves about on the platform deck. It was rather a tight squeeze for so many human beings in that space.

After greeting the submarine boys, Mr. Mayhew turned to the cadets, calling their attention to the lines and outer construction of the "Farnum." Then he turned to the three submarine boys, signing to them to crowd forward.

"These young gentlemen," announced the lieutenant commander, "are Mr. Benson, Mr. Hastings and Mr. Somers. All three are thoroughly familiar with the Pollard type of boat. As the Navy has purchased one Pollard boat, and may acquire others, it is well that you cadets should understand all the working details of the Pollard Submarine Company's crafts. A few of you at a time will now step into the conning tower, and Mr. Benson will explain to you the steering and control gear used there."

Half a dozen of the cadets managed to squeeze into the conning tower. Jack experienced an odd feeling, half of embarrassment, as he explained before so many attentive pairs of eyes. Then another squad of cadets took the place of the first on-lookers. After a while all had been instructed in the use of the conning tower appliances.

"Mr. Benson," continued the lieutenant commander, "will now lead the way for all hands to the cabin. There he will explain the uses of the diving controls, the compressed air apparatus, and other details usually worked from the cabin."

Down below came the cadets, in orderly fashion, without either haste or lagging. Having warmed up to his subject, Jack

Benson lectured earnestly, even if not with fine skill. At last he paused.

"Any of the cadets may now ask questions," announced Lieutenant Commander Mayhew.

There was a pause, then one of the older cadets turned to Jack to ask:

"What volume of compressed air do you carry at your full capacity?"

"Mr. Benson's present status," rapped Mr. Mayhew, quickly, "is that of a civilian instructor. Any cadet who addresses Mr. Benson will therefore say 'sir,' in all cases, just as in addressing an officer of the Navy."

The cadet so corrected, who was at least twenty-one years old, flushed as he glanced swiftly at sixteen-year-old Jack. To say "sir" to such a youngster seemed almost like a humiliation. Yet the cadet repeated his question, adding the "sir." Jack quickly answered the question. Then two or three other questions were asked by other cadets. It was plain, however, that to all of the cadets the use of "sir" to so young a boy appealed, at least, to their sense of humor.

Through the engine room door Sam Truax and Williamson stood taking it all in. Sam saw a flash in the eye of one big cadet when the question of "sir" came up.

Presently the squad filed into the engine room. Here Hal Hastings had the floor for instruction. He did his work coolly, admirably, though he asked Jack Benson to explain a few of the points.

Then the questions began, directed at Hal. This time none of the cadets, under the watchful eyes of Mr. Mayhew, forgot to say "sir" when speaking to Hastings.

Sam Truax edged up behind the big cadet whose eyes he had seen flash a few moments before.

"Go after Benson, good and hard," whispered Truax.

The cadet looked keenly at Truax.

"You can have a lot of fun with Benson," whispered Truax, "if you fire a lot of questions at him, hard and fast. Benson is a conceited fellow, who knows a few things about the boat, but you can get him rattled and red-faced in no time."

CHAPTER X

A SQUINT AT THE CAMELROORELEPHANT

The big cadet wheeled upon Jack.

"Mr. Benson, how long have you been engaged on submarine boats, sir?"

"Since July," Jack replied.

"July of this year?"

"Yes."

"And it is now October. Do you consider that enough time, sir, in which to learn much about submarine boats?"

"That depends," Skipper Jack replied, "upon a man's ability in such a subject."

"Is it long enough time, sir, for a boy?"

That was rather a hard dig. Instantly the other cadets became all attention.

"It depends upon the boy, as it would upon the man," Jack answered.

"Do you consider, Mr. Benson, that you know all about

88   Victor G. Durham

submarine boats, sir?"

"Oh, no."

"Who does, sir?"

"No one that I ever heard of," Jack answered. "Few men inte-rested in submarine boats know much beyond the peculiarities of their own boats."

"And that applies equally to boys, sir?"

"Yes," Jack smiled.

"Do you consider yourself, sir, fully competent to handle this craft?"

"I'd rather someone else would say it," Jack replied. "My employers, though, seem to consider me competent."

"What is this material, sir?" continued the cadet, resting a hand on a piston rod.

"Brass," Benson replied, promptly.

"Do you know the specific gravity and the tensile strength of this brass?"

Before Jack could answer Mr. Mayhew broke in, crisply:

"That will do, Mr. Merriam. Your questions appear to go beyond the limits of ordinary instruction, and to partake more of the nature of a cross-examination. Such questions take up the time of the instruction tour unnecessarily."

Cadet Merriam flushed slightly, as he saluted the naval officer. Then the cadet's jaws settled squarely. He remained silent.

A few more questions and the hour was up.

Lieutenant Commander Mayhew gave the order for the cadets to pass above and embark in the cutters. He remained behind long enough to say to the three submarine boys:

"You have done splendidly, gentlemen - far better than I expected you to do. If you manage the sea instruction as well, in the days to come, our cadets will have a first-class idea of the handling of the Pollard boats."

"I wish, sir," Jack replied, after thanking the officer, "that the cadets were not required to say 'sir' to us. It sounds odd, and I am quite certain that none of the young men like it."

"It is necessary, though," replied Mr. Mayhew. "They are required to do it with all civilian instructors, and it would never do to draw distinctions on account of age. Yes; it is necessary."

When the second squad of cadets arrived, in the afternoon, the three submarine boys found themselves ready for their task without misgivings. Eph took more part in the explanations than he had done in the forenoon. Then came a third squad of cadets, to be taken over the same ground. The young men of both these squads used the "sir" at once, having been previously warned by one of the naval officers.

"That will be all for to-day, Mr. Benson, and thank you and your friends for some excellent work," said Lieutenant Commander Mayhew, when the third squad had filed away.

"Say, for hard work I'd like this job right along," yawned Eph Somers, when the three were alone in the cabin. "Just talking three times a day - what an easy way of living!"

"It's all right for a while," agreed Jack. "But it would grow tiresome after a few weeks, anyway. Lying here in the Basin, and talking like a salesman once in a while, isn't like a life of adventure."

"Oh, you can sigh for adventure, if you wish," yawned Eph. "As for me, I've had enough hard work to appreciate a rest once in a while. Going into the town to-night, Jack?"

"Into town?" laughed the young skipper. "I went last night - and some of the folks didn't do a thing to me, did they?"

"Aren't you going to report the robbery to the police?" demanded Hal, opening his eyes in surprise.

"Not in a rush," Jack answered. "If I do, the police may start at once, and that mulatto and his friends, being on the watch, will take the alarm and get away. If I wait two or three days, then the mulatto's crowd will think I've dropped the whole thing. I reckon the waiting game will fool them more than any other."

"Yes, and all the money they got away from you will be spent," muttered Eph.

Jack, none the less, decided to wait and think the matter over.

Supper over, the submarine boys, for want of anything else to do, sat and read until about nine o'clock. Then Jack looked up.

"This is getting mighty tedious," he complained. "What do you fellows say to getting on shore and stretching our legs in a good walk?"

"In town?" grinned Eph, slyly.

Jack flushed, then grinned.

"No!" he answered quietly; "about the Academy grounds."

"I wonder if it would be against the regulations for a lot of rank outsiders like us to go through the grounds at this hour?"

"'Rank outsiders'?" mimicked Jack Benson, laughing. "You forget, Hal, old fellow, that we're instruct - hem! civilian instructors - here."

"I wonder, though, if it would be in good taste for us to go prowling through the grounds at this hour?" persisted Hal.

"There's one sure way to find out," proposed Benson. "We can try it, and, if no marine sentry chases us, we can conclude that we're moving about within our rights. Come along, fellows."

Putting on their caps, the three went up on the platform deck. The engine room door was locked and Williamson and Truax had already turned in. There was a shore boat at the landing. Jack sent a low-voiced hail that brought the boat out alongside.

"Will it be proper for us to go through the Academy grounds at this hour?" Jack inquired of the petty officer in the stern.

"Yes, sir; there's no regulation against it. And, anyway, sir, you're all stationed here, just now."

"Thank you. Then please take us ashore."

At this hour the walks through the grounds were nearly deserted. A few officers, and some of their ladies living at the naval station, were out. The cadets were all in their quarters in barracks, hard at study, or supposed to be.

For some time the submarine boys strolled about, enjoying the air and the views they obtained of buildings and grounds. Back at Dunhaven the air had been frosty. Here, at this more southern port, the October night was balmy, wholly pleasant.

"I wonder if these cadets here ever have any real fun?" questioned Eph Somers.

"I've heard - or read - that they do," laughed Hal.

"What sort of fun?"

"Well, for one thing, the cadets of the upper classes haze the plebe cadets a good deal."

"Humph! That's fun for all but the plebes. Who are the plebes, anyway?"

"The new cadets; the youngest class at the Academy," Hal replied.

"What do they do to the plebe?" Eph wanted to know.

"I guess the only way you could find that out, Eph, would be to join the plebe class."

"Reckon, when I come to Annapolis, I'll enter the class above the plebe," retorted Somers.

The three submarine boys had again approached the cadet barracks building.

"Here comes a cadet now, Eph," whispered Jack. "If he has the time, I don't doubt he'd be glad to answer any questions you may have for him."

Young Benson offered this suggestion in a spirit of mischief, hoping the approaching cadet, when questioned, would resent it stiffly. Then Eph would be almost certain to flare up.

The cadet, however, suddenly turned, coming straight toward them, smiling.

"Good evening, gentlemen," was the cadet's greeting.

"Good evening," was Jack's hearty reply.

"You've never been here before, have you, sir?"

"Never," Jack confessed.

"Then I take it you have never, sir, seen the camelroorelephant?"

"The cam -" began Eph Somers.

Then he stopped, clapping both hands to his right jaw.

"Won't you please hand that to us in pieces?" begged Eph, speaking as though with difficulty.

The cadet laughed heartily, then added:

"Don't try to pronounce it, gentlemen, until you've seen the camelroorelephant. It's a cadet joke, but it's well worth seeing. Shall I take you to it?"

"Why, yes, if you'll be good enough," Jack assented, heartily.

The cadet glanced quickly about him, then said in a low voice:

"This way, please, gentlemen."

He led the strangers quickly around the end of barracks to an open space in the rear. Here he halted.

"Gentlemen, I must ask you to close your eyes, and keep them closed, on honor, until I ask you to open them again. You won't have to keep your eyes closed more than sixty seconds before the camelroorelephant will be ready for inspection. Now, eyes closed, please."

Lingering only long enough to make sure that his request had been met, the cadet stole noiselessly away.

Nor was it many seconds later when all three of the submarine boys began to feel suddenly suspicious.

"I'm going to open my eyes," whispered Eph.

"You're on honor not to," warned Jack Benson, also in a whisper.

"I didn't give my word," retorted Eph, "and I'm going to - oh, great shades of Santiago!"

The very genuine note of concern in Eph's voice caused Jack and Hal to open their own eyes instantly.

Nor could any of the three repress a quick start.

From all quarters naval cadets were advancing stealthily upon them. Something in the very attitude and poise of the young men told the submarine boys that these naval cadets were out for mischief.

"We're in for it!" breathed Jack, in an undertone. "We're in for something real and startling, I reckon. Fellows, brace up and take your medicine, whatever it is, like men!"

CHAPTER XI

BUT SOMETHING HAPPENED!

Nor was Jack's guess in the least wrong.

Even had the submarine boys attempted to bolt they would have found it impossible. They were surrounded.

The cadets closed quickly in upon them. There were more than thirty of these budding young naval officers.

It was Cadet Merriam who stepped straight up to Jack, giving him a grotesque and exaggerated salute, as he rumbled out:

"Good evening, SIR!"

Like a flash Jack Benson comprehended. These cadets intended fully to even up matters for having been obliged to say "sir" to these very youthful "civilian instructors."

"Good evening," Jack smiled.

"You have come to see the camelroorelephant, SIR?"

"We've been told that we might have that pleasure," Jack responded, still smiling.

"Perhaps you may," retorted Cadet Merriam, "though, first of all, it will be necessary to prove yourselves worthy of the privilege, SIR."

"Anything within our power," promised Jack.

"Then, SIR, let me see you all three stand 'at attention.'"

"At attention" is the rigid attitude taken by a United States soldier or sailor when in the presence of his officers. Jack had already seen men in that attitude, and did his best to imitate it in smart military manner. Eph and Hal did likewise.

"No, no, no, you dense blockheads!" uttered Cadet Midshipman Merriam. "'At attention' upside down - on your hands!"

The other cadet midshipmen now hemmed in closely about the three. Jack thought he caught the idea. He bent over, throwing his feet up in the air and resting on his hands. Unable to keep his balance, he walked two or three steps.

"I didn't tell you to walk your post, blockhead!" scowled Mr. Merriam. "Stand still when at attention."

Jack tried, but of course made a ludicrous failure of standing still on his hands. So did Hal and Eph. The latter, truth to tell, didn't try very hard, for his freckled temper was coming a bit to the surface.

"You're the rawest recruits, the worst landlubbers I've ever seen," declared Cadet Midshipman Merriam, with severe dignity. "Rest, before you try it any further."

The smile had all but left Jack Benson's lips, though he tried to keep it there. Hal Hastings made the most successful attempt at looking wholly unconcerned. Eph's face was growing redder every minute. It is a regrettable fact that Eph was really beginning to want to fight.

"See here," ordered Mr. Merriam, suddenly, taking Jack by the arm, "you're a horse, a full-blooded Arab steed - understand!"

He gave young Benson a push that sent that youngster down to the ground on all fours.

"You're General Washington, out to take a ride on your horse," announced Mr. Merriam, turning to Hal. "It's a ride for your health. Do you understand? It will be wholly for your health to take that ride!"

Hal Hastings couldn't help comprehending. With a sheepish grin he sat astride of Jack Benson's back as the latter stood on all fours.

"Go ahead with your ride, General," called Mr. Merriam.

Jack pranced as best he could, on all fours, Hal making the load of his own weight as light as he could. Over the ground the pair moved in this nonsensical ride, the cadets following and grinning their appreciation of the nonsense.

Two of the young men followed, holding Eph by the arms between them. Mr. Merriam now turned upon the unhappy freckled boy.

"Down on all fours," ordered Mr. Merriam. "You're the measly dog that barked at General Washington on that famous ride. Bark, you wretched yellow cur - bark, bark, *bark*!"

Though Eph Somers was madder than ever, he had just enough judgment remaining to feel that the wisest thing would be to obey instructions. So, on all fours, Eph raced after Jack, barking at him.

"See how frightened the horse is," muttered one of the midshipmen.

Taking the hint, Jack shied as well as he could.

"That's all," said Mr. Merriam, at last. "All of that, at least."

Victor G. Durham

As the three submarine boys rose, each found himself gently held by a pair of cadet midshipmen. It was a more or less polite hint that the ordeal was not yet over. Mr. Merriam turned to whisper to one of the cadets, who darted inside the barracks building. He was back, promptly, carrying a folded blanket on his arm.

A grin spread over the faces of the assembled cadet midshipmen. The bearer of the blanket at once unfolded it. As many of the cadets as could got hold of the edges, bending, holding the blanket spread out over the ground.

Jack Benson's two captors suddenly hurled him across the length of the blanket with no gentle force. Instantly the cadets holding the blankets straightened up, jerking it taut. Up into the air a couple of feet bounded Jack. As his body came down the cadets holding the blanket gave it a still harder jerk. This time Jack shot up into the air at least four feet. It was the same old blanket-tossing, long popular both in the Army and Navy. Every time Jack landed the blanket was given a harder jerk by those holding it. Benson began to go higher and higher.

And now the cadets broke into a low, monotonous chant, in time to their movements. It ran:

Sir, sir, surcingle!
Sir, sir, circle!
Sir, sir, with a shingle -
Sir, sir, sir!

As regular as drumbeats the cadets ripped out the syllables of the refrain. At each word Jack Benson's body shot higher and higher. These young men were experts in the gentle art of blanket-tossing. Ere long the submarine boy was going up into the air some eight or nine feet at every tautening of the blanket.

As for escape, that was out of the question. No sooner did the submarine boy touch the blanket than he shot skyward again.

Had he desired to he could not have called out. The motion and the sudden jolts shook all the breath out of him.

"Ugh! Hm! Pleasant, isn't it?" uttered Hal Hastings, grimly, under his breath.

"If they try to do that to me," whispered Eph, hotly, under his breath, "I'll fight."

"More simpleton you, then!" Hal shot back at him in warning. "What chance do you think you stand against a crowd like this?"

Just as suddenly as it had begun the blanket-tossing stopped. Yet, hardly had Jack been allowed to step out than Hal Hastings was unceremoniously dropped athwart the blanket. The tossing began again, to the chant of:

Sir, sir, surcingle!
Sir, sir, circle!

Right plentifully were these cadet midshipmen avenging themselves for having had to say "sir" to these young submarine boys that day.

"Woof!" breathed Jack, as soon as breath entered his body again. Eph clenched his fists tightly, as Hal continued to go higher and higher. But at last Hastings's ordeal was over.

"I suppose they'll try that on me!" gritted Eph Somers to himself. "If they do -"

That was far as he got, for Eph was suddenly flung upon the blanket.

Sir, sir, surcingle!

Then how Eph *did* go up and down! It was as though these cadet midshipmen knew that it would make Eph mad, madder, maddest! These budding young naval officers fairly bent to their work, tautening and loosening on the blanket until their muscles fairly ached.

It was lofty aerial work that Eph Somers was doing. Up and up - higher and higher! Without the need of any effort on his own part young Somers was now traveling upward at the rate of ten or eleven feet at every punctuated bound.

Then, suddenly, there came a sound that chilled the blood of every young cadet midshipman hazer present.

"*Halt!* Where you are!"

Under the shadow of the barracks building a naval officer had appeared. He now came forward, a frown on his face, eyeing the culprits.

It is no merry jest for cadet midshipmen to be caught at hazing! And here were some thirty of them - red-handed!

CHAPTER XII

JACK BENSON, EXPERT EXPLAINER

At the first word of command from the officer several of the cadet midshipmen who were near enough to an open doorway vanished through it.

As the officer strode through the group of startled young men a few more, left behind his back, made a silent disappearance.

There were left, however, as the officer looked about him, sixteen of the young men, all too plainly headed and led by Cadet Midshipman Merriam.

"Young gentlemen," said the officer, severely, "I regret to find so many of you engaged in hazing. It is doubly bad when your victims are men outside the corps. And, if I mistake not, these young gentlemen are here as temporary civilian instructors in submarine work."

Mr. Merriam and his comrades made no reply in words. Nor did their faces express much. They stood at attention, looking stolidly ahead of them, though their faces were turned toward the officer. It was not the place of any of them to speak unless the officer asked questions.

Severe as the hazing had been, however, Jack and Hal, at least, had taken it all in good part. Nor was Jack bound by any of the rules of etiquette that prevented the cadets from speaking.

Victor G. Durham

"May I offer a word, sir?" asked Jack, wheeling upon the officer.

"You were one of the victims of a hazing, were you not?" demanded the officer, regarding Jack, keenly.

"Why, could you call it that, sir?" asked Jack, a look of innocent surprise settling on his face. "We called it a demonstration - an explanation."

"Demonstration? Explanation?" repeated the officer, astonished in his turn. "What do you mean, Mr. - er -?"

"Benson," Jack supplied, quietly.

"I think you would better tell me a little more, Mr. Benson," pursued the unknown naval officer.

"Why, it was like this, sir," Jack continued. "My two friends - Hastings and Somers - and myself were talking about the West Point and Annapolis hazings, of which we had heard and read. We were talking about the subject when a cadet came along. I suggested to Somers that we ask the cadet about hazing. Well, sir, to make a long story short, some of the cadets undertook to show us just how hazing is - or used to be - done at Annapolis."

"Oh! Then it was all thoroughly good-natured, all in the way of a joke, to show you something you wanted to know?" asked the naval officer, slowly.

"That's the way I took it," replied Jack. "So did Hastings and Somers. We've enjoyed ourselves more than anyone else here has."

This was truth surely enough, for, in the last two minutes, not one of the cadet midshipmen present could have been accused of *enjoying* himself.

"Then what took place here, Mr. Benson, really took place at your request?" insisted the naval officer.

"It all answered the questions that we had been asking," Jack replied, promptly, though, it must be admitted, rather evasively.

"This is your understanding, too, Mr. Hastings?" demanded the officer.

"Surely," murmured Hal.

"You, Mr. Somers?"

"I - I haven't had so much fun since the gasoline engine blew up," protested Eph.

"We entered most heartily into the spirit of the thing," Jack hastened on to say, "and feel that we owe the deepest thanks to these young gentlemen of the Navy. Yet, if our desire to know more about the life - that is, the former life - of the Academy is to result in getting our entertainers into any trouble, we shall never cease regretting our unfortunate curiosity."

For some moments the naval officer regarded the three submarine boys, solemnly, in turn. From them he turned to look over the cadet midshipmen. The latter looked as stolid, and stood as rigidly at attention, as ever.

"Under this presentation of the matter," said the officer, after a long pause, "I am not prepared to say that there has been any violation of discipline. At least, no grave infraction. However, some of these young gentlemen are, I believe, absent from their quarters without leave. Mr. Merriam?"

"I have permission to be absent from my quarters between nine and ten, sir."

"Mr. Caldwell?"

"Absent from quarters without permission, sir."

So on down through the list the officer ran. Nine of the young men proved to have leave to be away from their quarters. The other seven did not have such permission. The names of these seven, therefore, were written down to be reported. The seven, too, were ordered at once back to their quarters.

Having issued his instructions, the naval officer turned and walked away. Jack and his comrades, too, left the scene.

Yet they had not gone far when they heard a low hail behind. Turning, they saw Cadet Midshipmen Merriam hastening toward them.

"Gentlemen," he said, earnestly, as he reached them, "it may not be best for me to be seen lingering here to talk with you. But my comrades wanted me to come after you and to say that we think you bricks. You carried that off finely, Mr. Benson. None of us will ever forget it."

"It wasn't much to do," smiled Jack, pleasantly.

"It was quick-witted of you, and generous too, sir," rejoined Mr. Merriam, finding it now very easy to employ the "sir." "Probably you agree with us that no great crime was committed, anyway. But, just the same, hazing is under a heavy ban these days. If you hadn't saved the day as you did, sir, all of our cadet party might have been dismissed the Service. Those absent from quarters without leave will get only a few demerits apiece. We have that much to thank you for, sir, and we do. All our thanks, remember. Good night, sir."

"My courage was down in my boots for a while," confessed Hal Hastings, as the three chums continued their walk back to the Basin.

"When?" demanded Eph, grimly. "When your boots - and the rest of you - were so high up in the air over the blanket?"

"No; when the cadets were caught at it," replied Hal.

"Say, Jack," demanded Eph, "do you ever give much thought to the future life?"

"Meaning the life in the next world?" questioned Benson.

"Yes."

"I sometimes give a good deal of thought to it," Jack confessed.

"Then where do you expect to go, when the time comes?"

"Why?"

"After the whoppers you told that officer?"

"I didn't tell him even a single tiny fib," protested Jack, indignantly.

"Oh, you George Washington!" choked Eph Somers.

"Well, I didn't," insisted Jack. "Now, just stop and think. Weren't we all three discussing hazing?"

"Yes."

"Then that part of what I told the officer was straight. Now, Eph, when we saw that first cadet come along, didn't I suggest to you to ask him about hazing?"

"Ye-es," admitted Somers, thoughtfully.

"Then, didn't the cadet midshipmen offer to show us all about hazing pranks, and didn't they do it?"

"Well, rather," muttered Eph.

"Now, young man, that's all I told the officer, except that we

Victor G. Durham

enjoyed our entertainment greatly."

"*Did* we enjoy it, though?" demanded Eph Somers, bridling up.

"I did," replied Jack, "and I spoke for myself. I enjoyed it as I would enjoy almost any new experience."

"So did I," added Hal, warmly. "It was rough - mighty rough - but now I know what an Annapolis hazing is like, and I'm glad I do."

"Well, I want to tell you I didn't enjoy it," blazed Eph. "It was a mighty cheeky -"

"Then why did you let the officer imagine you enjoyed it?" taunted Jack.

While Hal put in, slyly:

"Eph, you're too quick to talk about others fibbing. From the evidence just put in, it's evident that you're the only one of the three who fibbed any. Won't you please walk on the other side of the road? I never did like to travel with liars."

"Oh, you go to Jericho!" flared Eph. But, as he walked along, he blinked a good deal, and did some hard thinking.

"I'll tell you," broke out Jack, suddenly, "who thanks us even more than the cadets themselves do."

"Who?" queried Hal.

"That officer who caught the crowd at it."

"Do you think he cared?"

"Of course he did," said Jack, positively. "He'd rather have gone hungry for a couple of days than have to report that bunch for hazing."

"Then why was he so infernally stiff with the young men?"

"He had to be; that's the answer. That officer, like every other officer of the Navy detailed here, is sworn to do his full duty. So he has to enforce the regulations. But don't you suppose, fellows, that officer was hazed, and did some hazing on his own account, when he was a cadet midshipman here years ago? Of course! And that's why the officer didn't question us any more closely than he did. He was afraid he might stumble on something that would oblige him to report the whole crowd for hazing. *He* didn't want to do it. That officer, I'm certain, knew that, if he questioned us too closely, he'd find a lot more beneath the surface that he simply didn't want to dig up."

"Would you have told the truth, if he had questioned you searchingly, and pinned you right down?" demanded Eph Somers.

"Of course I would," Jack replied, soberly. "I'm no liar. But I feel deeply grateful to that officer for not being keener."

Before nine o'clock the next morning news of the night's doings back of barracks had spread through the entire corps of cadet midshipmen.

With these young men of the Navy there was but one opinion of the submarine boys - that they were trumps, wholly of the right sort.

As a result, Jack, Hal and Eph had hundreds of new friends among those who will officer the Navy of the morrow.

Not so bad, even just as a stroke of business!

CHAPTER XIII

READY FOR THE SEA CRUISE

For the next ten days things moved along without much
excitement for the submarine boys.

During that time they had an average of four sections a day of
cadet midshipmen to instruct in the workings of the Pollard
type of submarine torpedo boat.

During the last few days short cruises were taken on the Severn
River, in order that the middies might practise at running the
motors and handling the craft. At such times one squad of
midshipmen would be on duty in the engine room, another in
the conning tower and on the platform deck.

Of course, when the midshipmen handled the "Farnum,"
under command of a Navy officer, the submarine boys had but
little more to do than to be on board. Certainly they were not
overworked. Yet all three were doing fine work for their
employers in making the Navy officers of the future like the
Pollard type of craft.

After waiting a few days Jack Benson reported to the Annapolis
police his experience with the mulatto "guide." The police
thought they recognized the fellow, from the description, and
did their best to find him. The mulatto, however, seemed to
have disappeared from that part of the country.

There came a Friday afternoon when, as the last detachment of middies filed over the side into the waiting cutter, Lieutenant Commander Mayhew announced:

"This, Mr. Benson, completes the instruction desired in the Basin and in the river. To-morrow and Sunday you will have for rest. On Monday, at 10 A.M., a section will report aboard for the first trip out to sea. Then you will show our young men how the boat dives, and how she is run under water. As none of our cadet midshipmen have ever been below in a submarine before, you will be sure of having eager students."

"And perhaps some nervous ones," smiled Skipper Jack.

"Possibly," assented Mr. Mayhew. "I doubt it, though. Nervousness is not a marked trait of any young man who has been long enrolled at the Naval Academy."

"Can we have a slight favor done us, Mr. Mayhew?" Jack asked.

"Any reasonable favor, of course."

"Then, sir, we'd like to spend a little time ashore, as we've been confined so long aboard. If I lock up everything tight on the boat until Sunday night, may we know that the 'Farnum' will be under the protection of the marine guard?"

"I feel that there will not be the slightest difficulty in promising you that," replied Mr. Mayhew. "I will telephone the proper authorities about it as soon as I go on shore."

All hands on board were pleased over the prospect of going ashore, with the exception of Sam Truax.

"You don't need any guard on the boat," he protested. "I don't want to go ashore. Leave me here and I'll be all the guard necessary."

"We're all going ashore," Jack replied.

"But I haven't any money to spend ashore," objected Truax.

"I'll let you have ten dollars on account, then," replied Jack, who was well supplied with money, thanks to a draft received from Jacob Farnum.

"I don't want to go ashore, anyway."

"I'm sorry, Truax, but it doesn't really make any difference. The boat will be closed up tight, and there wouldn't be any place for you to stay, except on the platform deck."

"You're not treating me fairly," protested Sam Truax, indignantly.

"I'm sorry you think so. Still, if you're not satisfied, all I can do is to pay you off to date. Then you can go where you please."

"I'm here by David Pollard's order. Do you forget that?"

"He sent you along to us, true," admitted Jack, "but I have instructions from Mr. Farnum to dismiss anyone whose work on board I don't like. Now, Truax, you're a competent enough man in the engine room, and there's no sense in having to let you go. You're well paid, and can afford the time on shore. I wouldn't make any more fuss about this, but do as the rest of us are going to do."

"Oh, I'll have to, then, since you're boss here," grumbled Truax, sulkily.

"I don't want to make it felt too much that I *am* boss here," Jack retorted, mildly. "At the same time, though, I'm held responsible, and so I suppose I'll have to have things done the way that seems best to me."

Sam Truax turned to get his satchel. The instant his back was turned on the young commander Sam's face was a study in ugliness.

"Oh, I'll take this all out of you," muttered the fellow to himself. "I don't believe, Jack Benson, you'll go on the cruising next week. If you do, you won't be much good, anyway!"

Ten minutes later a shore boat landed the entire party from the submarine craft.

"Going with the rest of us, Truax?" inquired Jack, pleasantly.

"No; I'm going to find a boarding-house. That will be cheaper than the hotel."

So the other four kept straight on to the Maryland House, giving very little more thought to the sulky one.

It was not until after supper that Eph turned the talk back to Sam Truax.

"I don't like the fellow, at all," declared young Somers. "He always wants to be left alone in the engine room, for one thing."

"And I've made it my business, regular," added Williamson, the machinist, "to see that he doesn't have his wish."

"He's always sulky, and kicking about everything," added Eph. "I may be wrong, but I can't get it out of my head that the fellow came aboard on purpose to be a trouble-maker."

"Why, what object could he have in that?" asked Captain Jack.

"Blessed if I know," replied Eph. "But that's the way I size the fellow up. Now, take that time you were knocked senseless, back in Dunhaven. Who could have done that? The more I think about Sam Truax, the more I suspect him as the fellow who stretched you out."

"Again, what object could he have?" inquired Benson.

"Blessed if I know. What object could anyone have in such a trick against you? It was a state prison job, if the fellow had been caught at the time."

"Well, there's one thing Truax was innocent of, anyway," laughed Captain Jack. "He didn't have any hand in the way I was tricked and robbed by the mulatto."

"Blamed if I'm so sure he didn't have a hand in that, too," contended Eph Somers, stubbornly.

"Yet Mr. Pollard recommended him," urged Jack.

"Yes, and a fine fellow Dave Pollard is - true as steel," put in Hal Hastings, quietly. "Yet you know what a dreamer he is. Always has his head in the air and his thoughts among the stars. He'd as like as not take a fellow like Truax on the fellow's own say-so, and never think of looking him up."

"Oh, we've no reason to think Truax isn't honest enough," contended Jack Benson. "He's certainly a fine workman. As to his being sulky, you know well enough that's a common fault among men who spend their lives listening to the noise of great engines. A man who can't make himself heard over the noise of a big engine hasn't much encouragement to talk. Now, a man who can't find much chance to talk becomes sulky a good many times out of ten."

"We'll have trouble with that fellow, Truax, yet," muttered Eph.

"Oh, I hope not," Jack answered, then added, significantly:

"If he *does* start any trouble he may find that he has been trifling with the wrong crowd!"

Very little more thought was given to the sulky one. The submarine boys and their companion, Williamson, enjoyed Saturday and Sunday ashore.

All of them might have felt disturbed, however, had they known of one thing that happened.

The naval machinists aboard the first submarine boat, the "Pollard," now owned by the United States Government, found something slightly out of order with the "Pollard's" engine that they did not know exactly how to remedy.

Sam Truax, hanging around the Basin that Sunday forenoon, was called upon. He gladly responded to the call for help. For four hours he toiled along in the "Pollard's" engine room. Much of that time he spent there alone.

The job done, at last, Truax quietly received the thanks of the naval machinists and went ashore again.

Yet, as he turned and walked toward the main gate of the grounds, there was a smile on Sam Truax's face that was little short of diabolical.

"Now, if I can only get the same chance at the 'Farnum's' engines!" he muttered, to himself. "If I can, I think Mr. Jack Benson will find himself out of favor with his company, for his company will be out of favor with the Navy Department at Washington!"

CHAPTER XIV

THE "POLLARD" GOES LAME

"The submarine boats when out in the Bay will keep abreast of the 'Hudson,' two hundred yards off on either beam. The speed will be fourteen knots when the signal is given for full speed. The general course, after leaving the mouth of the Bay will be East."

Such were the instructions called from the rail of the gunboat, through a megaphone, Monday forenoon.

On each of the submarine craft were sixteen cadet midshipmen, out for actual practice in handling a submarine in diving and in running under water. On board the gunboat were eighty more cadets. Thus a large class of the young men were to receive instruction during the cruise, for the detachments aboard the submarines could be changed at the pleasure of Lieutenant Commander Mayhew, who was in charge of the cruise.

Captain Jack, his own hands on the conning tower wheel, ran the "Farnum" out into the river, first of all. Then the "Pollard," under command of a naval officer, followed. Both backed water, then waited for the "Hudson" to come out, for the gunboat was to lead the way until the Bay was reached. Then the formation ordered would be followed.

Though it was nearing the first of November, the day, near

land, was ideally soft and balmy. As many of the midshipmen as could sought the platform deck of the "Farnum." Those, however, who belonged to the engineer division were obliged to spend the greater part of their time below.

By the time that the three craft were in the ordered formation, abreast, and well started down Chesapeake Bay, the parent vessel signaled that the designated cadets were to take charge of the handling of the submarine boats.

Jack Benson cheerfully relinquished the wheel to Cadet Midshipman Merriam, and stepped out on to the platform deck. At need, as in case of accident or misunderstanding of signals or orders, Benson was still in command. While all ran smoothly, however, Mr. Merriam enjoyed command.

Hal, being likewise relieved in the engine room, came also out on deck.

"Where's Eph?" inquired the young commander of the "Farnum."

"In the engine room," smiled Hal. "He said I could leave, if I wanted, but that he'd be hanged if he'd let Truax out of his sight while I was away."

"Eph seems to have Truax on the brain," laughed Jack.

"Well, Truax *is* a queer and surly one," Hal admitted. "This morning he gives one the impression of peeking over his shoulder all the time to see whether he's being watched."

"So Eph means to humor him by watching him, eh?" asked Jack.

Hal laughed quietly.

Some of the cadets who were familiar with the landmarks of Chesapeake Bay pointed out many of the localities and sights to the two submarine boys.

At last, however, Eph was obliged to call for Hal.

"You know, Hal, old fellow, I've got to look out for the feeding of a lot of boarders to-day," complained Eph, whimsically.

This task of Eph's took time, though it was not a hard one. The food for the cadets had been sent aboard. Eph had to make coffee and heat soup. For the rest, cold food had to do. The young men, on this trip, were required to wait on themselves.

Hal found Sam Truax sitting moodily in a corner of the engine room, though there was something about the fellow's appearance that suggested the watchfulness of a cat.

"Why don't you go on deck a while, Truax?" asked Hal, kindly.

"Don't want to," snapped the fellow, irritably. So Hal turned his back on the man.

"Doesn't that part need loosening up a bit, sir?" asked the cadet in charge of the engineer division.

"Yes," replied Hastings, after watching a moment; "it does."

"I'll do it, then," proposed Truax, roughly. He attempted to crowd his way past Hal, but the latter refused to be crowded, and stood his ground until the midshipman passed him a wrench. Then Hastings loosened up the part.

"You might let me do a little something," growled Sam Truax, in a tone intentionally offensive.

"Don't forget, Truax, that I'm in command in this department," retorted Hal, in a quieter tone than usual, though with a direct, steady look that made Sam Truax turn white with repressed wrath.

"You won't let me forget it, will you?" snarled the fellow.

"No; for I don't want you to forget it, and least of all on this cruise," responded Hal Hastings.

"You don't give me any chance to -"

"Silence!" ordered Hal, taking a step toward him.

Sam Truax opened his mouth to make some retort, then wisely changed his mind, dropping back into his former seat.

The noon meal was served to all hands. By the time it was well over the mouth of the Bay was in sight, the broad Atlantic rolling in beyond.

The sea, when reached, proved to be almost smooth. It was ideal weather for such a cruise.

Then straight East, for an hour they went, getting well out of the path of coasting vessels.

"Hullo! What in blazes does that mean?" suddenly demanded Hal, pointing astern at starboard.

The "Pollard" lay tossing gently on the water, making no headway. Hardly ten seconds later the "Hudson" signaled a halt.

Then followed some rapid signaling between the gunboat and the submarine that had stopped. There was some break in the "Pollard's" machinery, but the cause had not yet been determined.

"Blazes!" muttered Jack, uneasily. "It couldn't have happened at a worse time. This looks bad for our firm, Hal!"

The "Farnum" now lay to, as did the "Hudson," for the officer in command of the "Pollard" signaled that his machinists were making a rapid but thorough investigation of the unfortunate submarine's engines.

Finally, a cutter put off from the "Hudson," with a cadet midshipman in charge. The small boat came over alongside, and the midshipman called up:

"The lieutenant commander's compliments, and will Mr. Benson detail Mr. Hastings to go over to the 'Pollard' and assist?"

"My compliments to the lieutenant commander," Jack replied. "And be good enough to report to him, please, that Mr. Hastings and I will both go."

"My orders, sir, are to convey you to the 'Pollard' before reporting back to the parent vessel," replied the midshipman.

The cutter came alongside, taking off the two submarine boys, while Eph Somers devoted himself to watching Sam Truax as a bloodhound might have hung to a trail.

Arrived on board the good, old, familiar "Pollard," Jack and Hal hurried below.

"The machinery is too hot to handle, now, sir," reported one of the naval machinists, "but it looks as though something was wrong right in there" - pointing.

"Put one of the electric fans at work there, at once," directed Hal. "Then things ought to be cool enough in half an hour, to make an examination possible."

After seeing this done, the two submarine boys left for the platform deck, for the engine room was both hot and crowded.

"How long is it going to take you, Mr. Hastings?" asked the

naval officer in command of the "Pollard."

"Half an hour to get the parts cool enough to examine, but I can't say, sir, how long the examination and repairs will take."

So the officer in command signaled what proved to be vague and unsatisfactory information to Lieutenant Commander Mayhew.

"This is a bad time to have this sort of thing happen," observed the naval officer in charge.

"A mighty bad time, sir," Jack murmured.

"And the engines of the 'Pollard' were supposed to be in first-class condition."

"They *were* in A-1 condition, when the boat was turned over to the Navy," Jack responded.

"Do you imagine, then, Mr. Benson, that some of the naval machinists have been careless or incompetent?"

"Why, that would be a wild guess to make, sir, when one remembers what high rank your naval machinists take in their work," Jack Benson replied.

"And this boat was sold to the Navy with the strongest guarantee for the engines," pursued the officer in charge.

Jack and Hal were both worried. The sudden break had a bad look for the Pollard boats, in the success of which these submarine boys were most vitally interested.

At last, from below, the suspected parts of the engine were reported to be cool enough for examination. The naval officer in charge followed Jack and Hal below.

Taking off his uniform blouse and rolling up his sleeves, Hal sailed in vigorously to locate the fault. Machinists and cadets stood about, passing him the tools he needed, and helping him when required.

At last, after disconnecting some parts, Hal drew out a long, slender brass piston.

As he held it up young Hastings's face went as white as chalk.

"Do you see this?" he demanded, hoarsely.

"Filed, crazily, and it also looks as though the inner end had been heated and tampered with," gasped Jack Benson.

"This, sir," complained Hal, turning around to face the naval officer in charge, "looks like a direct attempt to tamper with and damage the engine. Someone has done this deliberately, sir. It only remains to find the culprit."

"Then we'll find out," retorted the naval officer, "if it takes a court of inquiry and a court martial to do it. But are you sure of your charge, Mr. Hastings?"

"Am I sure?" repeated Hal, all the soul of the young engineer swelling to the surface. "Take this piston, sir, and examine it. Could such a job have been done, unless by sheer design and intent?"

"Will the lieutenant permit me to speak?" asked the senior machinist, taking a step forward and saluting.

"Yes; go ahead."

"Yesterday morning, sir," continued the senior machinist, "we thought the engines needed some overhauling by someone more accustomed to them than we were. We saw one of the machinists of the 'Farnum,' sir, hanging about on shore. So we invited him aboard and asked him to look the engines over."

"Describe the man," begged Jack.

The senior machinist gave a description that instantly denoted Sam Truax as the man in question.

"Did you leave him alone in here, at any time?" demanded Hal.

"Let me see. Why, yes, sir. The man must have been alone in here some three-quarters of an hour."

Jack and Hal exchanged swift glances.

There seemed, now, very little need of carrying the investigation further.

CHAPTER XV

ANOTHER TURN AT HARD LUCK

When he could trust himself to speak Hal Hastings addressed the naval officer.

"I think Mr. Benson and myself understand, sir, how it happened that this damage was done. There are extra parts in the repair kit. In twenty minutes, sir, I think we can have the engines running smoothly once more."

The naval officer was wise enough not to press the questioning further just then. Instead, he went on deck.

Working like beavers, and with the assistance of others standing about, Jack and Hal had the piston replaced and all the other parts in place within fifteen minutes. Then, once more, Hal turned on the gasoline, set the ignition, and watched.

The engine ran as smoothly as ever.

"There won't be any more trouble, unless someone is turned loose here with files and a blast lamp," pronounced Hal. Then he and his chum sought the deck, to report to the officer in charge.

"You think we're in running order, now?" asked that officer.

"If you give the speed-ahead signal, sir, I think you'll feel as though you had a live engine under your deck," Hal assured him.

The signal was given, the "Pollard" immediately responding. She cut a wide circle, at good speed, returning to her former position, where the propellers were stopped.

"You suspect your own machinist, who was aboard?" asked the naval officer, in a low tone, of the submarine boys.

"If you'll pardon our not answering directly, sir," Captain Jack replied, "we want to have more than suspicions before we make a very energetic report on this strange accident. But we shall not be asleep, sir, in the matter of finding out. Then we shall make a full report to Mr. Mayhew."

"Success to you - and vigilance!" muttered the naval officer.

The gunboat's cutter came alongside, transferring Jack and Hal back to the "Farnum."

Hal went directly below to the engine room.

"You fixed the trouble with the 'Pollard'?" demanded Eph Somers, eagerly.

"Yes," Hal admitted.

"What was wrong?"

"Why, I don't know as I'd want to commit myself in too offhand a way," replied Hal, slowly, as though thinking.

"What appeared to be at the bottom of the trouble?"

"Why, it *may* have been that one of the naval machinists, not understanding our engines any too well, allowed one of the pistons to get overheated, and then resorted to filing,"

Hal replied.

"What? Overheat a piston, and then try to correct it with a file?" cried young Somers, disgustedly. "The crazy blacksmith! He ought to be set to shoeing snails - that's all he's fit for."

"It looks that way," Hal assented, smiling.

Artful, clever Hal! He had carried it all off so coolly and naturally that Sam Truax, who had been closely studying Hastings's face from the background, was wholly deceived.

"This fellow, Hastings, isn't as smart as I had thought him," muttered Truax, to himself.

The interrupted cruise now proceeded, the parent vessel signaling for a temporary speed of sixteen knots in order to make up for lost time.

Twenty minutes later came the signal from the "Hudson:"

"At the command, the submarines will dash ahead at full speed, each making its best time. During this trial, which will end at the firing of a gun from the parent vessel, all cadets will be on deck."

Word was immediately passed below, and all the cadets of the engineer division came tumbling up.

To these, who had been in the engine room constantly for hours, the cool wind blowing across the deck was highly agreeable.

For the speed dash Captain Jack Benson had again taken command. He passed word below to Eph Somers to take the wheel in the conning tower.

Eph, therefore, came up with the last of the cadets from below. In the excitement of the pending race it had not been noticed by any of the submarine boys that Williamson was already on deck, aft. That left Sam Truax below in sole possession of the boat's engine quarters.

The gunboat now fell a little behind, leaving the two submarines some four hundred yards apart, but as nearly as possible on a line.

"Look at the crowd over on the 'Pollard's' decks," muttered Hal. "They're all Navy folks over there."

"And they mean to beat such plain 'dubs' as they must consider us," laughed Captain Jack, in an undertone.

"Will they beat us, though?" grinned Hal Hastings. "You and I, Jack, happen to know that the 'Farnum' is a bit the faster boat by rights."

Suddenly the signal broke out from the gunboat.

"Race her, Eph!" shouted Captain Jack.

"Aye, aye, sir!"

Eph Somers's right hand caught at the speed signals beside the wheel. He called for all speed, the bell jangling merrily in the engine room.

A little cheer of excitement went up from the cadets aboard the "Farnum" as that craft shot ahead over the waters. The cadets were catching the thrill of what was virtually a race. At the same time, though, these midshipmen could not help feeling a good deal of interest in the success of the "Pollard," which was manned wholly by representatives of the Navy.

In the first three minutes the "Farnum" stole gradually, though slowly, ahead of the "Pollard." Then, to the disgust of all three of the submarine boys, the other craft was seen to be gaining. Before long the "Pollard" had the lead, and looked likely to increase it. Already gleeful cheers were rising from the all-Navy crowd on the deck of the other submarine.

Behind the racers sped the "Hudson," keeping just far enough behind to be able to observe everything without interfering with either torpedo craft.

From looking at the "Pollard" Captain Jack glanced down at the water. His own boat's bows seemed to be cutting the water at a fast gait. The young skipper, knowing what he knew about both boats, could not understand this losing to the other craft.

"The Navy men must know a few tricks with engines that we haven't guessed," he observed, anxiously, to young Hastings.

"I don't know what it can be, then," murmured Hal, uneasily. "There aren't so confusingly many parts to a six-cylinder gasoline motor. They aren't hard engines to run. More depends on the engine itself than on the engineer."

"But look over there," returned Captain Jack Benson. "You see the 'Pollard' taking the wind out of our teeth, don't you?"

"Yes," Hal admitted, looking more puzzled.

"Do you think our engines are doing the top-notch of their best?" asked Benson.

"Yes; for Williamson is a crackerjack machinist. He knows our engines as well as any man alive could do."

"Do you think it would do any good for you to go below, Hal?"

"I will, if you say so," offered Hastings. "Yet there's another side to it."

"What?"

"Williamson might get it into his head that I went below because I thought he was making a muddle of the speed. As a matter of fact, he knows every blessed thing I do about our motors, and Williamson is loyal to the core."

"I know," nodded Captain Jack. "I'd hate to hurt a fine fellow's feelings. Yet - confound it, I *do* want to win this burst of speed. It means, perhaps, the quick sale of this boat to the Navy. If we're beaten it means, to the Secretary of the Navy, that he already has our best boat, and he might not see the need of buying the 'Farnum' at all."

"Give Williamson two or three minutes more," begged Hal. "You might tell Eph, though, to repeat, and repeat, the signal for top speed. That'll show Williamson we're losing."

Jack Benson walked to the conning tower, instructing Eph Somers in a low tone.

"I've signaled twice, since the first time," Eph replied. "But here goes some more."

"I wonder what's going wrong with our engines, then," muttered Captain Jack, uneasily.

"It ain't in careless steering, anyway," grumbled Eph. "I'm going as straight as a chalk line."

"I noticed that," Captain Jack admitted.

He continued to look worried, for, by this time, the "Pollard" was at least a good two hundred and fifty yards to the good in the lead.

"I'm afraid," muttered Hal, rejoining Benson, "that I'll simply have to go below."

"I'm afraid so," nodded Jack. "We simply can't afford to lose this or any other race to the 'Pollard.'"

"Williamson knows that fully as well as we do, though," Hal Hastings went on. "And Williamson -"

Of a sudden Hal stopped short. He half staggered, clutching at a rail, while his eyes stared and his lips twitched.

"Why - why - there's Williamson - aft on the deck!" muttered Hastings.

"What!"

Jack, too, wheeled like a flash. Back there in a crowd of cadets stood the machinist upon whom the submarine boys were depending for the best showing that the "Farnum" could make.

"Williamson up here!" gasped Hal. "And -"

"That fellow, Truax, all alone with the motors!" hissed Captain Jack. Then, after a second or two of startled silence:

"Come on, Hal!"

The naval cadets were too much absorbed in watching the race to have overheard anything. Williamson, too, standing at the rail, looking out over the water, had not yet discovered that Hal Hastings was up from the engine room.

Jack Benson stole below on tip-toe, though with the machinery running so much stealth was not necessary. Right behind him followed Hal.

As the two gained the doorway of the engine room Sam Truax had his back turned to them, and so did not note the sudden watchers.

There was a smile of malicious triumph on Truax's face as he turned a lever a little way over, thus decreasing the ignition power of the motors.

Both Jack and Hal could see that the gasoline flow had been turned on nearly to the full capacity. It was the poor ignition work that was making the motors respond so badly. A little less, and a little less, of the electric spark that burned the gasoline and air mixture - that was the secret of the gradually decreasing speed, while all the time it looked as though the "Farnum" was doing her level best to win the race.

Whistling, as he bent over, Sam Truax caught up a long, slender steel bar. With this he stepped forward, intent upon his next wicked step.

"Gracious! The scoundrel is going to run that bar in between the moving parts of the engine and bring about a break-down!" quivered Hal.

Sam Truax stood watching for his chance to thrust the steel bar in just where it would inflict the most damage. Then raising the bar quickly, he poised for the blow.

"Stop that, you infernal sneak!" roared Jack Benson, bounding into the engine room.

CHAPTER XVI

BRAVING NOTHING BUT A SNEAK

"You - here?" hissed Truax, wheeling about.

He had not had time to make the thrust with the steel bar.

Instead, as he wheeled, he raised it above his head, drawing back in an attitude of guard.

As he did so, a vile oath escaped Truax's lips.

"Put that bar down!" commanded Jack Benson, standing unflinchingly before the angry rascal.

"I'll put it down on your head, if you don't get out of here!" snarled the wretch.

"Put it down, and consider yourself off duty here, for good and all," insisted Jack.

"Are you going to get out of here, or shall I brain you?" screamed Truax, his face working in the height of his passion.

"Neither," retorted Captain Jack, coolly. "I command here, and you know it. Put that bar down, and leave the engine room."

"Come and take the bar from me - if you dare!" taunted the

fellow, a more wicked gleam flashing in his eyes.

"Hal!" called Jack, sharply.

"Aye!"

"Call two or three of the cadets down here. Don't make any noise about it."

This order was called without Benson's turning his head. He still stood facing the sneak while Hal sped away.

"Now, I've got you alone!" gloated Truax. "I'll finish you!"

A scornful smile curled Jack's lips as he gazed steadily back at his foe.

"Truax, you're a coward, as well as a sneak."

"I am - eh?"

With another nasty oath Truax stepped quickly forward, the steel bar upraised.

He took but one step, however, for Captain Jack Benson had not retreated an inch.

Nor did Jack have his hands up in an attitude of guard.

"Are you going to put that bar down, Truax?" the young skipper demanded, in a voice that betrayed not a tremor.

"No."

"Then you'll have to make good in a moment, for we're going to attack you."

"Bah! I can stave in two or three heads before any number of you could stop me," sneered the fellow, in an ugly voice.

Victor G. Durham

"You could, but you won't dare."

"I won't?"

"Not you!"

At that instant rapid steps were heard. Hal Hastings returned with three of the midshipmen, behind them Williamson trying to crowd his way into the scene.

"Just tell us what you want, Mr. Benson," proposed Cadet Merriam, amiably.

"This fellow has been 'doping' our engines," announced Captain Jack. "And now he's threatening to stand us off. We'll close in on him from both sides. If he tries to use that steel bar on any of us -"

"If he does, he'll curse his unlucky star," declared Midshipman Merriam. "Come on, gentlemen. We'll show him some of the Navy football tactics!"

The three midshipmen approached Truax steadily from the right. Jack, Hal and Williamson stepped in on the left.

With a yell like that of a maniac Sam Truax swung the bar.

Having to watch both sides at once, however, he made a fizzle of it. The bar came down, but struck the floor.

Then, with a yell, the midshipmen leaped in on one side, Jack leading the submarine forces on the other. Mr. Merriam's trip and Jack's smashing blow with the fist brought Truax down to the floor in a heap.

"Now, cart this human rubbish out of here!" ordered Jack Benson, sternly. "Don't hit him - he isn't man enough to be worthy of a blow!"

Swooping down upon the prostrate one, Hal and the midshipmen seized Sam Truax by his arms and legs, carrying him bodily out of the engine room.

"Williamson," commanded Captain Jack, "stop the speed."

"In the race, sir. We -"

"Stop the speed," repeated Benson.

"You're the captain," admitted Williamson. Grasping the twin levers of the two motors he swung them backward.

"Disregard any signal to go ahead until we've had a chance to inspect the motors," added Captain Jack.

Then the submarine skipper darted out into the cabin.

Sam Truax lay sprawling on the floor. Midshipman Merriam, a most cheerful smile on his face, sat across the fellow, while Hal and the other two midshipmen stood by, looking on.

"Hold him please, until I can have the wretch taken care of," requested Captain Jack, making for the spiral stairway to the conning tower.

Just as the young skipper stepped out on deck he heard the "Hudson's" bow-gun break out sharply in the halting signal.

Taking a megaphone, Benson stood at the rail until the gunboat ranged up alongside.

"Have you broken down?" came the hail from the gunboat's bridge.

"I thought it best to stop speed, sir. We'll have to look over our engines before it will be safe to attempt any more speed work," Captain Jack answered. "I've caught a fellow tampering with our machinery. We hold him a prisoner, now. Can you take him off our hands, sir?"

"One of *your own* men?" came back the question.

"Of course, sir."

"We'll send a marine guard to take him, on your complaint, Mr. Benson."

"Thank you, sir."

The gunboat's engines slowed down. Ere long her port side gangway was lowered. Jack saw not only two marines and a corporal come down over the side, but Lieutenant Commander Mayhew appeared in person. That officer came over in the cutter.

"You've had treachery aboard, have you?" asked the lieutenant commander, as he climbed up over the side.

"Rather. A new machinist, taken aboard just before we sailed from Dunhaven. The same fellow who must have played the trick on the 'Pollard's' engines yesterday," Benson replied.

"I'll be glad to have a fellow like that in irons in the brig aboard the 'Hudson,' then," muttered Mr. Mayhew. "I couldn't understand, Mr. Benson, how you were doing so badly in the full speed ahead dash."

"The prisoner below is the answer, sir," Captain Jack replied. He then led the corporal and two marines below. The corporal produced a pair of handcuffs, which he promptly snapped over Truax's wrists.

"You'll be sorry for this, one of these days," threatened Truax, with a snarl that showed his teeth.

"Some day, then, if you please, when I have more leisure than I have now," Jack retorted, dryly. "This man is all yours, corporal."

Truax was foolish enough to try to hang back on his conductors. A slight jab through the clothing from one of the marines' bayonets caused the prisoner to stop that trick. He was taken on deck and over the side.

"Coxswain, return for me after you've taken the prisoner to the 'Hudson,'" directed Mr. Mayhew. "Now, Mr. Benson, I would like to see what has been done to your engines."

"That's just what I want to know, too," responded Jack.

They found Hal and Williamson hard at work, inspecting the motors.

"The ignition power was lowered, and that may have been the most that the fellow did," said Hal. "Yet, at the same time, before putting these engines to any severe test, I believe they ought to be cooled and looked over."

Lieutenant Commander Mayhew frowned.

"These delays eat up our practice cruise time a whole lot," he grumbled.

"I'll put the engines through their paces, and chance mischief having been done to them, if you wish, sir."

"No; that won't do either, Mr. Hastings," replied the naval officer. "This craft is private property, and I have no right to give orders that may damage private property. I'll hold the fleet until you've had time to inspect your engines properly. By that time, however, we'll have to put back to the coast for the night, for our practice time will be gone."

"In the days to follow, sir," put in Benson, earnestly, "I think we can more than make up for this delay. We won't have the traitor aboard after this."

"What earthly object can the fellow have had for wanting to damage your motors?" demanded the naval officer, looking hopelessly puzzled.

"I can't even make a sane guess, sir," Jack Benson admitted.

An hour and a half later the "Hudson" and the two submarines headed back for a safe little bay on the coast. Here the three craft anchored for the night.

CHAPTER XVII

THE EVIL GENIUS OF THE WATER FRONT

It was nearly eight in the evening when the three craft were snug at anchor.

The bay was a small one, hardly worthy of the name. The only inhabited part of the shore thereabouts consisted of the fishing village known as Blair's Cove, a settlement containing some forty houses.

Hardly had all been made snug aboard the "Farnum" when Jack, standing on the platform deck after the cadets had been transferred to the "Hudson" for the night, saw a small boat heading out from shore.

"Is that one of the new submarine crafts?" hailed a voice from the bow of the boat.

"Yes, sir," Jack answered, courteously.

No more was said until the boat had come up alongside.

"I thought maybe you'd be willing to let me have a look over a craft of this sort," said the man in the bow. He appeared to be about forty years of age, dark-haired and with a full, black beard. The man was plainly though not roughly dressed; evidently he was a man of some education.

Victor G. Durham

"Why, I'm mighty sorry, sir," Captain Jack Benson replied. "But I'm afraid it will be impossible to allow any strangers on board during this cruise."

"Oh, I won't steal anything from your craft," answered the stranger, laughingly. "I won't be inquisitive, either, or go poking into forbidden corners. Who's your captain?"

"I am, sir."

"Then you'll let me come aboard, just for a look, won't you?" pleaded the stranger.

Such curiosity was natural. The man seemed like a decent fellow. But Jack shook his head.

"I'm sorry, sir, but I'm positive our owners wouldn't approve of our allowing any strangers to come on board."

"Had any trouble, so far, with strangers?" asked the man.

"I didn't say that," Jack replied, evasively. "But the construction of a submarine torpedo boat is a secret. It is a general rule with our owners that strangers shan't be allowed on board, unless they're very especially vouched for. Now, I hate to appear disobliging; yet, if you've ever been employed by anyone else, you will appreciate the need of obeying an owner's orders."

"You're under the orders of the boss of that gunboat?" asked the stranger, pointing to the "Hudson."

"On this cruise, yes, sir," Jack nodded.

"Maybe, if I saw the fellow in command of the gunboat, then he'd give me an order allowing me to come on board."

"I'm very certain the lieutenant commander wouldn't do anything of the sort," Benson responded.

The stranger gave a comical sigh.

"Then I'm afraid I don't see a submarine boat to-night - that is, any more than I can see of it now."

"That's about the way it looks to me, also," Jack answered, smiling. "Yet, believe me, I hate awfully to seem discourteous about it."

"Oh, all right," muttered the stranger, nodding to the two boatmen, who had rowed him out alongside.

"Good!" grunted Eph. "I'm glad you didn't let him on board, Captain. On this cruise our luck doesn't seem to run with strangers."

"It doesn't, for a fact," laughed Jack Benson.

"Hi, ho - ah, hum!" yawned young Somers, stretching. "It will be mine for early bunk to-night, I reckon."

At this moment a boat was observed rounding the stern of the "Hudson." It came up alongside, landing a marine sentry.

"Anybody on the 'Farnum' want to go ashore to-night?" hailed a voice from the gunboat's rail. "The shore boat will be ready in five minutes."

"I believe I would like to take just a run through the village," declared Jack, turning to his chum. "Do you feel like a land-cruise with me, Hal?"

"I think I'd better go," laughed Hastings. "You seem to get into trouble when you go alone."

"All right, then. And, Eph since you're so sleepy, you can turn in as soon as you want. The boat will be under sufficient protection," Jack added, nodding toward the marine slowly pacing the platform deck.

Williamson was called too, but declared that he felt like turning in early. So, when the shore boat came, it had but two passengers to take from the submarine. There were a few shore-leave men, however, from the gunboat.

"This boat will return to the fleet, gentlemen, every hour up to midnight," stated the petty officer in charge, as Jack and Hal stepped ashore at a rickety little wharf.

"Judging from what we can see of the town from here, we'll be ready to go back long before midnight," Jack Benson laughingly told his companion.

"All I want is to shake some of the sea-roll out of my gait," nodded Hastings. "It surely doesn't seem to be much of a town."

By way of public buildings there turned out to be a church, locked and dark, a general store and also a drug-store that contained the local post-office. But the drug-store carried no ice cream or soda, so the submarine boys turned away.

There was one other "public" place that the boys failed to discover at once. That was a low groggery at the further end of the town. Here two of the sailors who had come on shore leave turned in for a drink or two. They found a suave, black-bearded man quite ready to buy liquor for Uncle Sam's tars.

Three-quarters of an hour later Jack and Hal felt they had seen about as much of the town as they cared for, when a hailing voice stopped them.

"Finding it pretty dull, gentlemen?"

"Oh, good evening," replied Captain Jack, recognizing the bearded man whom he had refused admittance to the "Farnum."

"Pretty stupid town, isn't it, Captain?" asked the stranger, holding out his hand, which Jack Benson took.

"As lively as we thought it would be," Hal rejoined. "We just came ashore to stretch ourselves a bit. Thought we might lay a course to an ice-cream soda, too, but failed."

"These fishermen don't have such things," smiled the stranger. "They are content with the bare necessities of life, with a little grog and tobacco added. Speaking of grog, would you care to try the best this town has, gentlemen?"

"Thank you," Jack answered, politely. "We've never either of us tasted the stuff, and we don't care to begin."

"Drop into the drug-store and have a cigar, then?"

"We don't smoke, either, thank you," came from Hal.

"You young men are rather hard to entertain in a place like this," sighed the stranger, but his eyes twinkled.

"We are just as grateful for the intention," Jack assured him.

"Tell you what I can do, gentlemen," proposed the stranger, suddenly. "I might invite you down to my shack for a little while, and show you my books and some models of yachts and ships that I've been collecting. I'm quite proud of my collection in that line. Won't you come?"

Anything in the line of yacht or ship-models interested both of these sea-loving boys from the shipyard at Dunhaven. Jack graciously accepted the invitation for them both.

"And, though I have no soda fountain," continued the bearded one, "I can offer you some soft drinks. I always keep some about the place."

"How do you come to be living in a place like this, if I'm not too inquisitive?" queried Benson, as the three strolled down

Victor G. Durham

the street.

"Doctor's orders," replied the bearded one. "So I've rented the best old shack I could get here, down by the water. I spend a good deal of my time sailing a sloop that I have. Curtis is my name."

Jack and Hal introduced themselves in turn.

Curtis's shack proved to be well away from the village proper, and down near the waterfront. A light shone from a window near the front door as the three approached the small dwelling.

"I think I can interest you for an hour, gentlemen," declared the bearded one, as he slipped a key in the lock of the door.

He admitted them to a little room off the hallway, a room that contained not much beyond a table and four chairs, a side-table and some of the accessories of the smoker.

"Just take a seat here," proposed Curtis, "while I get some sarsaparilla for you. I'll be right back in a moment."

It was four or five minutes before Curtis came back, bearing a tray on which were three tall glasses, each containing a brownish liquid.

"The stuff isn't iced, yet it's fairly cold," the bearded one explained. "Well, gentlemen, here's to a pleasant evening!"

Hal, who was thirsty, took a long swallow of the sarsaparilla, finding the flavor excellent. Jack drank more slowly, though he enjoyed the beverage.

"If you don't mind," suggested Curtis, "I will light a cigar. And say, by the way, gentlemen, what if we take a little walk down to my beach? Before showing you the models I spoke of, I'd like to have your opinion of the lines of my sloop."

"We'll go down and take a look with great pleasure," Jack Benson agreed, rising. "And I'm glad, sir, that you're able to show us more courtesy than we were able to offer you to-night."

"Oh, that was all right," declared their host, smiling good-humoredly. "Rules are rules, and you have your owners to please. No hard feelings on that score, I assure you."

Curtis led the way through a dark yard down to a pier. Moored there lay a handsome white sloop, some forty-two feet in length - a boat of a good and seaworthy knockabout type.

"This is a sloop, all right," Jack agreed, cordially. "Rather different from the lumbering fishing craft hereabouts."

"Oh, hah, yum!" yawned Hal, at which Curtis shot a quick glance at him.

"Come on board," invited Curtis, stepping down to the deck of the craft. "Let me show you what a comfortable cruising cabin I have."

"Hi, oh, yow!" yawned Hal, again. "Jack, I think I shall enjoy my rest to-night."

"Same case here," agreed Benson, stifling a yawn that came as though in answer to Hal's.

"I won't keep you long, gentlemen, if I am boring you," agreed their host, amiably. "Now, I'll go below first and light up. So! Now, come down and take a look. Do you find many yacht cabins more comfortable than this one?"

It was, indeed, a cozy place. Up forward stood a miniature sideboard, complete in every respect with glass and silver. In the center of the cabin was a folding table. There were locker seats and inviting looking cushions. The trim was largely of mahogany. On either side was a broad, comfortable-looking berth.

"Just get into that berth and try it, Mr. Hastings," urged the bearded one.

"I - I'm afraid to," confessed Hal, stifling another yawn.

"Afraid?"

"Very sure thing!"

"Why?"

"I'm - hah-ho-hum!" yawned Hal Hastings. "I'm afraid I'd - yow! - abuse your hospitality by going to sleep."

Jack Benson leaned against the edge of the opposite berth, feeling unaccountably drowsy.

"Oh, nonsense," laughed Curtis. "Just pile into that berth for a moment, Hastings, and see what a soft, restful place it is. I'll agree to pull you out, if necessary."

Not realizing much, in his approaching stupor, Hal Hastings allowed himself to be coaxed to stretch himself at full length in the downy berth.

Almost immediately he closed his eyes, drifting off into stupor.

"Why, your friend *is* drowsy, isn't he?" laughed the bearded one, turning to the submarine skipper.

Jack Benson's own eyelids were suspiciously close together.

"Why - what - ails you?"

Curtis spoke in a low, droning, far-away voice that caused Jack Benson's upper eyelids to sink. Curtis stood watching him, in malicious glee, for some moments. Then, at last, he took hold of the young skipper.

"Come, old fellow," coaxed the bearded one, "you'll do best to join your friend in a good nap. Get up in the berth."

"Lemme alone," protested the boy, thickly, feeling that he was being lifted. Jack struggled, partly rousing himself.

"Come, get up into the berth. You'll be more comfortable there."

"Lemme alone. What are you trying to do?" demanded Jack, swinging an arm.

Curtis dodged the light blow, then gripped Jack Benson resolutely.

"Now, see here, young man," hissed the bearded one, "I'm not going to have any more nonsense out of you. Up into the berth you go! Do you want me to hit you?"

Another man thrust his head down the cabin hatchway, showing an evil, grinning face.

"Got 'em right?" demanded the one from the hatchway.

"Yes," snapped the bearded one, then turned to give his attention to Jack Benson, who was putting up an ineffectual fight while Hal slumbered on. "Now, see here, Benson, quit all your fooling!"

"You lemme up," insisted the submarine boy, in a low, dull voice, though he swung both his arms in an effort to assert himself. "'M not goin' t' stay here. Lemme up, I say! 'M goin' back to - own boat."

"The submarine?" jeered the bearded man.

"Yep."

"Guess again, son," laughed Curtis, jeeringly. "You're not going back aboard the submarine to-night."

"Am so," declared Benson, obstinately, though his tone was growing more drowsy every instant, and his busy hands moved almost as weakly as an infant's.

"Listen, if you've got enough of your senses left," growled the bearded men. "You're not going back to the 'Farnum' - neither to-night, nor at any other time during the next few months. You're bound on a long cruise, but not on a submarine boat. I am the captain here, and I'll name the cruise!"

CHAPTER XVIII

HELD UP BY MARINES

It was barely a minute afterward that Jack Benson lapsed into a very distinct snore.

"No more trouble from this pair," laughed the bearded one to his companion at the hatchway. "Now, I'll douse the cabin light, and then we'll cast off. This thing has moved along very slickly."

Eph, after having made up his mind to turn in early, had found his sleepy fit passing. He read for a while in the cabin, then pulled on a reefer and went up on deck. Williamson was already in a berth, sound asleep.

"It would be a fine night if there was a moon," Eph remarked to the marine sentry on deck.

"Yes, sir."

The marine - "soldier, and sailor, too" - not being there for conversational purposes, continued his slow pacing, his rifle resting over his right shoulder.

As Eph strolled about in the limited space of the platform deck he heard a distant creaking. It was a sound that he well knew - the hoisting of sail.

Victor G. Durham

"I wonder if the local fishermen start out at this time of the night?" Eph Somers remarked, musingly, to the sentry.

"It may be so, sir; I don't know," replied the marine.

Presently Eph made out the lines and the spread of canvas of a handsome knockabout sloop standing on out of the harbor.

The course being narrow, the sloop was obliged to sail rather close to the fleet.

"That's no fisherman!" muttered Somers, watching, his hands thrust deep in his pockets.

Presently the sloop's hull was lost to Eph's sight beyond the gunboat. Then the boy heard a voice from the "Hudson's" deck roar out:

"Look alive, you lubber! Do you want to foul our anchor chain?"

"No, sir," came from the sloop's deck. "We'll clear you all right."

"See that you do, then!"

Then the sloop's hull came into view again, as the craft headed out toward the open water beyond.

"That's the kind of a craft Jack would give a heap to be on," thought Eph. "Queer that he should spend all his time on gasoline peanut-roasters when he's so fond of whistling for a breeze behind canvas."

As the sloop neared the mouth of the little bay, and her lines became rather indistinct in the darkness, Eph Somers turned to resume his pacing of the deck.

"Hullo," muttered the submarine boy, two or three minutes

later. "Here's the shore boat coming on its regular trip. I wonder if Jack and Hal are in it? It's about time for them to be coming on board."

But the shore boat, instead of coming out to the submarine, lay in at the side gangway of the gunboat opposite, and Eph discovered that his two comrades were not in the boat.

"I say," hailed Eph, "have you seen Mr. Benson and Mr. Hastings on shore!"

"No, sir," replied the petty officer in charge.

Then one of the sailors in the boat spoke in an undertone.

"This man says, sir," continued the petty officer, "that he saw your friends, sir, going aboard a white knockabout sloop."

"He did, eh?" demanded the astonished Eph. "How long ago was that?"

"Only a few minutes ago, sir," replied the sailor.

"You're sure you saw Mr. Benson and Mr. Hastings?"

"Yes, sir."

"That's queer," reflected Eph. "It wouldn't be like them to go sailing at this time of the night, and without notifying me, either. But, then, I didn't see anything of 'em aboard that sloop, either."

Eph was silent for a few moments, thinking. Then, suddenly, he leaped up in the air, coming down flat-footed.

"Crackey!" ejaculated Eph Somers.

For a moment or two his face was a study in bewilderment.

"Mighty strange things have been happening all through this cruise," Eph muttered, half-aloud. "Especially happening to Jack! Now, the two of them go aboard that sloop, and immediately after the boat puts out to sea in the dead of night. What if Jack and Hal have been shanghaied on that infernal sloop?"

Cold chills began to chase each other up and down the spine of Eph Somers. He was not, ordinarily, an imaginative youth, but just now the gruesome thought that had entered his mind persisted there.

He began to pace the platform deck in deep agitation.

"Anything wrong, sir?" questioned the marine sentry, halting and throwing his rifle over to port arms.

"That's just what I'd give a million dollars and ten cents to know!" exploded Eph.

"Gunboat, ahoy!" he shouted, some twenty seconds later.

"'Farnum,' ahoy!"

"I half believe, sir," Eph rattled on, "that my two comrades, Mr. Benson and Mr. Hastings have been tricked, in some way, and carried out to sea on that knockabout. They'd have been back from shore by this time, if nothing had happened."

"What do you want to do, Mr. Somers?"

"Want to do, sir?" retorted Eph. "I know what I'm going to do. I'm going to slip moorings and chase after that knock-about. What I wish to know from you, sir, is whether you'll send another marine or two on board, so that I can back up my demand to find my friends?"

"I'll have to ask the lieutenant commander about that, Mr. Somers."

"Can you do it, now, sir?" asked Eph, energetically.

"Instantly. I'll let you know the decision as soon as it's made."

Eph, hanging at the rail in the silence that followed, had no notion of whether his request had been a correct one. All he knew was that his suspicions had surged to the surface, and were threatening to boil over. It was a huge relief to the boy when Mr. Mayhew's voice sounded from the rail of the gunboat. Somers swiftly answered all questions.

"Your craft and crew are in a measure under our protection and orders," decided Mr. Mayhew. "I think we may properly extend you some help. I will send some men to you, and a cadet midshipman who will have my instructions."

"Will you send them quickly, sir?" begged Eph.

"I'll have men on board of you by the time that your engines are running," promised the lieutenant commander.

"Engines?" That word came as a fortunate reminder to the submarine boy. He darted below, almost yanking Williamson from his berth, nearly pulling the machinist into his clothes. By the time that Williamson was really wide awake he found himself standing by the motors forward.

Then young Somers darted onto deck again, just in time to see the boat coming alongside. It brought two more marines, one of them a corporal. There were also two sailors. A cadet midshipman commanded them.

"Mr. Somers," reported the cadet midshipman, "I am not intended to displace you from the command of this boat. I am here only with definite instructions in case you succeed in overhauling that white sloop."

"What -" began Eph. Then he paused, with a half-grin. "Really," he added, "I ought to know better than to quiz you about your instructions from your superior officer."

"Yes, sir," assented the midshipman, simply.

Eph turned on the current to the search-light, swinging the ray about the bay. Then, too impatient to sit in the conning tower, the submarine boy took his place by the deck wheel.

"Will your seamen cast loose from the moorings?" Somers asked.

"Yes, sir," replied the midshipman.

"If there's anything wrong, good luck to you," sounded the cool voice of Lieutenant Commander Mayhew, from the gunboat's rail.

"Thank you, sir."

No sooner had the moorings been cast loose from than Eph sounded the slow speed ahead bell. Within sixty seconds the propellers of the "Farnum" were doing a ten-knot stunt, which was soon increased to fourteen.

One of the seamen now stood by to swing the searchlight under Eph's orders.

By the time that the submarine reached the mouth of the bay the light faintly picked up a spread of white sail, off to the East.

"That's the knockabout," cried Eph, excitedly. "Now, see here, keep that ray right across the boat as soon as we get half a mile nearer."

"It'll show the boat that you're chasing 'em, sir," advised the midshipman.

"I know it," admitted Eph. "But it will also keep the rascals from dumping my friends overboard without our catching 'em at it."

"What do you think the men in charge of that boat are, sir - pirates?"

"They're mighty close to it, if they've shanghaied Mr. Benson and Mr. Hastings and put to sea with 'em," rejoined Eph. Then he rang for more speed. Down below, Williamson almost instantly responded. The "Farnum" now fairly leaped through the water.

"Turn the light on the knockabout, now, and keep it there," directed the submarine boy.

There was a seven-knot breeze blowing. At the speed at which the submarine boat was traveling the distance was soon covered.

And now the searchlight revealed two men in the standing-room of the sloop, one of whom, a bearded man, was looking backward over his wake much of the time.

"Can one of the marines fire a shot to stop those fellows?" asked Eph Somers.

"In the air, do you mean, sir?" asked the midshipman. "Certainly."

"Then I wish he'd do it."

Bang! The discharge of the rifle sounded sharply on the night air.

"It ain't stopping 'em any," muttered Eph, after a few seconds had gone by.

"Nothing would, unless fired into them," volunteered Midshipman Terrell.

It did not take long, however, to run the submarine up alongside of the sloop, at a distance of about one hundred yards.

"Now, we want you men to stop," called Midshipman Terrell, between his hands. "We are United States naval forces, from the gunboat, and you will regard this as an order that you must obey. No!" thundered the midshipman, suddenly, as the bearded one started to step down into the cabin. "You will both keep on deck. Otherwise we shall be obliged to fire into you. We mean business, remember!"

"What do you want to board us for?" demanded Curtis, pausing.

"We will explain when we come aboard."

"How are you coming, aboard? You've no small boat."

"We can land this submarine right up beside you," responded the midshipman, "if you keep straight to your present course."

"And scrape all the paint off our side," objected Curtis.

"That has no bearing on my instructions, sir. I direct you to keep straight to your present course. We will come up alongside."

"What if we don't do it?" demanded Curtis, with sudden bluster.

"Then your danger will be divided between being shot where you stand and having your craft cut in two by the bow of our craft," retorted Mr. Terrell. "You will realize, I think, that there can be no parleying with our orders."

The bearded one swore, but the corporal and his two marines stood at the rail with their rifles ready, waiting only the midshipman's order to aim and fire.

Eph allowed the "Farnum" to fall back a little way. Then he exerted himself to show his best in seamanship as he ran the submarine up to board the sloop by the starboard quarter. The two boats barely touched. Mr. Terrell, his three marines and two seamen leaped to the standing room of the yacht. Eph, all aquiver, let the nose of the "Farnum" fall back slightly. Then he trailed along, under bare headway.

Then a shout came from the sloop, as the two seamen reappeared, bearing the forms of Jack and Hal.

"We've found them aboard, Mr. Somers," shouted Terrell. "Drugged, I think, sir. Will you come alongside, sir."

Eph quickly rang the signal, then did some careful manoeuvring. As he touched, one of the marines leaped back to the platform deck, then passed a line to Mr. Terrell. The two craft were held together until Jack and Hal had been passed, still unconscious, over the side. The naval party quickly followed, then cast loose from the sloop.

"This whole proceeding is high-handed," growled Curtis, as soon as he saw that he was not to be molested.

"Oh, you shut up, and keep your tongue padlocked," retorted Midshipman Terrell, in high disgust. "You're lucky as it is. Now, Mr. Somers, are you going back to the bay, sir?"

"Aren't you going to take those two - body-snatchers?" demanded Eph, glaring venomously at the pair on the sloop.

"My instructions don't cover that, sir," replied the cadet midshipman.

"Then hang your orders!" muttered young Somers, but he kept the words behind his teeth. Eph veered off, next headed about, while the two seamen bore Jack and Hal below to their berths.

"Will you take the wheel, Mr. Terrell?" asked Eph, edging

away, with one hand on the spokes.

"Yes, sir."

Eph hurried below to the port stateroom. Jack lay in the lower berth, Hal in the upper. The two seamen, after feeling for pulse, stood by looking at the unconscious submarine boys.

"What's been done to them?" demanded Eph.

"The same old knockout drops, sir, that sailors in all parts of the world know so well, sir, I think," answered one of the men, with a quiet grin.

"Humph!" gritted Eph, bending over Jack's face. "Smell his breath."

"Yes, sir," said the sailor, obeying.

"There's no smell of liquor, there, is there?"

"No, sir," admitted the sailor, looking up, rather puzzled.

"There is some infernally mean trick in all this," growled Eph. "I am mighty sorry we didn't bring those rascals back with us."

When he went on deck again the submarine boy relieved Mr. Terrell at the wheel, completing the run in to moorings.

"Did you find your comrades aboard the sloop, Mr. Somers?" hailed the lieutenant commander, from the gunboat.

"Yes, sir."

"Are they all right?"

"Drugged, sir."

"Hm! Mr. Terrell and his detachment will return to this vessel."

The boat took them away. It was five minutes later when the boat returned, bringing the lieutenant commander, Doctor McCrea, the surgeon, and a sailor belonging to the hospital detachment aboard the "Hudson." Eph conducted them below.

"Drugged," announced the medical officer, after a brief examination.

"Humph!" uttered Mr. Mayhew. "That sort of trick isn't played on folks in any decent resort on shore. I don't understand Mr. Benson's conduct. I remember his mishap at Dunhaven. I remember the plight he got into at Annapolis; and now he and Mr. Hastings are found in this questionable shape. I am very much afraid these young men do not conduct themselves, on shore, in the careful manner that must be expected of civilian instructors to cadets."

Eph Somers felt something boiling up inside of him.

CHAPTER XIX

THE LIEUTENANT COMMANDER'S VERDICT

"Let me try to get at your meaning, sir, if you please," begged Somers, after standing for a few seconds with clenched fists. "Do you mean that my friends have been going into tough resorts on shore?"

"Where else do sailors usually get drugged?" inquired Mr. Mayhew. "What kind of people usually feed sea-faring men with what are generally known as knock-out drops?"

"How should I know?" demanded Eph, solemnly.

"You see your friends, and you see their condition."

"Smell their breaths, sir. There isn't a trace of the odor of liquor."

The surgeon did so, confirming Eph's claim.

"But I remember that Mr. Benson came aboard, at Dunhaven, with a very strong odor of liquor," continued the lieutenant commander.

"That had been sprinkled on his clothes, sir," argued Somers.

"Perhaps. But then there was the Annapolis affair."

"Mr. Benson explained that to you, sir."

"It's very strange," returned the lieutenant commander, "that such things seem to happen generally to Mr. Benson when he gets on shore. I know I have been ashore, in all parts of the world, without having such things happen to me."

"There is something behind this, sir, that doesn't spell bad conduct on the part of either of my friends," cried Eph, hotly. "There's some plot, some trick in the whole thing that we don't understand. And we might understand much more about it, sir, if your midshipman had arrested that pair of blackguards on the sloop, and brought them back with us."

"Had Mr. Benson and Mr. Hastings been members of the naval forces we could have done that," replied Mr. Mayhew. "Probably you don't understand, Mr. Somers, how very careful the Navy has to be about making arrests in times of peace, when the civil authorities are all-supreme. We carried our right as far as it could possibly be stretched when we boarded and searched that sloop for you."

"I don't care so much about that," contended Eph, warmly. "But it does jar on me, sir, to have you take such a view of my friends. You don't know them; you don't understand them as Mr. Farnum and Mr. Pollard do."

"Perhaps you wouldn't blame me as much for my opinions," replied Mr. Mayhew, "if you could look at the matter from my viewpoint, Mr. Somers. I am in charge of this cruise, which is one of instruction to naval cadets, and I am in a very large measure responsible for the conduct and good behavior of young men who have been selected as instructors to the cadets. If you were in my place, Mr. Somers, would you be patient over young men who, when they get ashore, get into one unseemly scrape after another? Or would you wonder, as I do, whether it will not be best for me to end this practice cruise and sail back to Annapolis, there to make my report in the matter?"

"For heaven's sake don't do that," begged Eph Somers, hoarsely. "At least, not until you have talked with Mr. Benson and Mr. Hastings. You'll wait until morning, sir?"

"I'm afraid I shall have to, if I want to talk with your friends," replied the lieutenant commander, smiling coldly. "And now, Mr. Somers, you and I had better leave here. The doctor and his nurse will want the room cleared in order to look after their patients. I hope your friends will be all right in the morning," added the naval officer, as the pair gained the deck.

"Now, see here, sir," began Eph, earnestly, all over again. "I hope you'll soon begin to understand that, whatever has happened, there are no two straighter boys alive than Jack Benson and Hal Hastings."

"I trust you're right," replied Mr. Mayhew, less coldly. "Yet, what can you expect me to think, now that Benson has been in such scrapes three different times? And, in this last instance, he drags even the quiet Mr. Hastings into the affair with him."

"I see that I'll have to wait, sir," sighed Eph, resignedly.

"Yes; it will be better in every way to wait," agreed the lieutenant commander. "It is plain justice, at the least, to wait and give the young men a chance to offer any defense that they can."

"Now, of course, from his way of looking at it, I can't blame him so very much," admitted Eph Somers, as he leaned over the rail, watching Mr. Mayhew going back through the darkness. "But Jack - great old Jack! - having any liking at all for mixing up in saloons and such places on shore! Ha, ha! Ho, ho!"

Williamson, now able to leave his motors, came on deck, asking an account of what had happened. The machinist listened in amazement, though, like Eph, he needed no proof that the boys, whatever trouble they had encountered, had met honestly and innocently.

"Of course that naval officer is right, too, from his own limited point of view," urged Williamson.

"Oh, yes, I suppose so," nodded Somers, gloomily. "I've been trying to tell myself that. But it would be fearful, wouldn't it, if the 'Farnum' were ordered away from the fleet, and Jack disgraced, just because of things he really didn't do."

"It's a queer old world," mused the machinist, thoughtfully. "We hear a lot about the consequences of wrong things we do. But how often people seem to have to pay up for things they never did!"

"Oh, well," muttered Eph, philosophically, "let's wait until morning. A night's sleep straightens out a lot of things."

Williamson, however, having had some sleep earlier in the night, was not drowsy, now. He lighted a pipe, lingering on the platform deck. Eph, not being a user of tobacco, went below to find that Doctor McCrea, from the gunboat, was sitting in the cabin, reading a book he had chosen from the book-case.

"I've brought the young men around somewhat," reported the physician. "I've made them throw off the drug, and now I've left some stuff with the nurse to help brace them up. They'll have sour stomachs and aching heads in the morning, though."

"But you noticed one thing, Doctor?" pressed Somers.

"What was that?"

"That there were no signs of liquor about them? Those boys never tasted a drop of the vile stuff in their lives!"

"I'm inclined to believe you," nodded the surgeon. "They have splendid, clear skins, eyes bright as diamonds, sound, sturdy heart-beats, and they're full of vitality. I've met boys from the slums, once in a while - beer-drinkers and cigarette-smokers. But such boys never show the splendid physical condition that your friends possess."

"You know, then, as well as I do, Doctor, that neither of my chums are rowdies, and that, whatever happened to them to-night, they didn't get to it through any bad habits or conduct?"

"I'm much inclined to agree with you, Mr. Somers."

"I hope, then, you'll succeed in impressing all that on Lieutenant Commander Mayhew in the morning."

With that the submarine boy passed on to the starboard state-room. He would have given much to have stepped into the room opposite, but felt, from the doctor's manner, that the latter did not wish his patients disturbed.

Eph slept little that night. Though Jack and Hal fared better in that single respect, Somers looked far the best of the three in the morning.

Jack and Hal came out with bandages about their heads, which buzzed and ached.

The two, however, told their story to Somers and Williamson as soon as possible.

"Just as I supposed," nodded Eph, vigorously.

"Why, how did you guess it all?" asked Benson, in astonishment.

"I mean, I knew you hadn't been in any low sailor resorts."

"Who said we had?" demanded Jack, flaring in spite of his dizziness.

"Some of the Navy folks didn't know but you had," replied Eph, then bit his tongue for having let that much out of the bag.

Doctor McCrea came aboard early. He looked the boys over.

"Eat a little toast, if you want, and drink some weak tea," he suggested. "After that, eat nothing more until to-night."

"But the day's work - ?" hinted Jack.

"I don't know," replied the doctor, shrugging his shoulders. "I'm not a line officer, and therefore know nothing about the fleet's manoeuvres."

That reply, however, was quite enough to send Jack Benson's suspicions aloft.

"Eph," he cried, wheeling upon his friend the moment Doctor McCrea was gone, "there's something you haven't told us."

"Such as - what?" asked Somers, doing his best to look mighty innocent.

"Doctor McCrea as good as admitted that we won't have anything to do to-day. What's wrong?" Then, after a brief pause: "Good heavens, does Mr. Mayhew believe we've been acting disgracefully? Are we barred out of the instruction work?"

Hal had been raising a glass of cold water to his lips. The glass fell, with a crash. He wheeled about, then clutched at the edge of the cabin table, most unsteadily.

"We-e-ll," admitted Somers, reluctantly, "Mr. Mayhew said he would want to question you some, perhaps, this morning."

"What did he say? Out with it all, Eph!"

A moment before Jack Benson had been pallid enough. Now, two bright, furious spots burned in either cheek.

The red-haired boy, however, was spared the pain of going any further, for, at that moment, a heavy tread was heard on the spiral staircase. Then Lieutenant Commander Mayhew, holding himself very erect, one hand resting against the scabbard of the sword that he wore at his side, came into view below.

Many were the questions that the naval officer put to the victims of the night's mishap.

"Well, gentlemen," Mr. Mayhew said at last, rising, "your story is strange. Yet, I believe you are young men of honor. I'm sorry we have not in custody the men who sailed that sloop."

"Pardon me, sir!" burst out Eph.

"Well, Mr. Somers?"

"Perhaps, sir, if you should question Truax you could learn something from him. I tell you, sir, there's a scheme to ruin Jack Benson; and that's only part of a bigger plot to discredit our company with the Navy!"

Mr. Mayhew, looking thoughtful, replied:

"I'll find some way of questioning Truax. And now, Mr. Benson, since you and Mr. Hastings are not fit to instruct the cadets to-day, I'll send out sections under Lieutenant Halpin on board the 'Pollard' only. To-morrow you should be in shape to resume your duties. Meanwhile, I must make one condition."

"It will not be necessary, sir, to make any conditions with us," Jack replied. "Your instructions will be sufficient."

"While you are on this present tour of duty, I shall ask Mr.

Benson and Mr. Hastings not to leave the 'Farnum' without my consent."

As soon as Mr. Mayhew had left the "Farnum" Eph Somers cried bitterly:

"You heard the verdict in the case! A great verdict! Not guilty - but don't do it again!"

At half past eight the next morning a section of cadets, under the command of Ensign Trahern, came aboard the "Farnum."

"The lieutenant commander sends word, with his compliments," reported Trahern, "that after leaving the bay the formation will be as usual. The signal to halt and be ready for the tour of instruction will be given when we're about ten miles off shore."

Six of the cadets, of the engineer division, went below to the engine room. To one of the ten left on deck Jack turned and said:

"You will take charge, Mr. Surles. Assume all the responsibilities of the officer of the deck."

In all, five of the midshipmen had commanded briefly before the laying-to signal was given. Hal Hastings then appeared on deck.

"Captain Benson," Hal stated, saluting, "I have inspected all the submerging machinery, and I find everything in good order. We can go below the surface at any time."

"Thank you, Mr. Hastings. All below!" ordered Jack crisply.

After the cadets and the ensign had filed below, Jack, having seen that all was in order, followed. He made all fast in the conning tower, then called Midshipman Surles up the stairway to the tower wheel.

"Do you think you can head due east and keep to that course under water, Mr. Surles?"

"Yes, sir."

Going down to the cabin floor, Jack ordered two more midshipmen to the tower as observers.

"The rest crowd about me and ask questions while I handle the submerging machinery."

Under the impetus from the electric motors, the propeller shafts began to throb. The next instant the submarine shot below, going down at so steep an angle that many of the middies were forced to reach for new footing.

"The gauge registers sixty feet below," announced Jack.

In another moment, by the quick flooding of some of the compartments astern, the young skipper brought the boat to an even keel.

Having finished the prescribed distance under water, Captain Jack turned on the compressed air to expel the water from the compartments. The conning tower soon rose above the water, and a moment later the "Pollard" also emerged.

Other cadets were transferred from the gunboat to the submarines, and the instruction proceeded. The manoeuvers for the day were ended with a half-hour run under water.

"By the way, sir, did you question Truax to see what you could learn about his reasons for acting as he did on the 'Farnum'?" asked Jack Benson the next day. Jack and Doctor McCrea were talking with Mr. Mayhew.

"I had him before me last night, and again this morning," replied Mr. Mayhew. "He said he hadn't an idea what I meant, and that is all I could get out of him."

Jack looked thoughtfully at Doctor McCrea for a moment before he exclaimed:

"Doctor, if I had anything like your chance, I'd have Sam Truax talking!"

"How?" Doctor McCrea looked interested.

"Why, I'd -" Jack hesitated, glancing toward the gunboat's commanding officer.

"I'd better go and see how the midshipmen are doing," laughed Mr. Mayhew, rising.

For some minutes Jack talked with Doctor McCrea. As the medical officer listened, he grinned, then laughed unrestrainedly.

"Mr. Benson, you're certainly ingenious!"

"Will you do what I've suggested?"

"Why, I - er - er -" Doctor McCrea hesitated. "I - well, I'll think it over." Again Doctor McCrea roared with laughter.

Victor G. Durham

CHAPTER XX

CONCLUSION

Sam Truax sat in the brig, between decks on the "Hudson," his scowling face turned toward the barred door, when the marine guard, taking a turn, peered in.

"Good heavens, man! What ails you?" demanded the marine.

"I'm all right," growled the prisoner.

"I'll be hanged if you look it."

"What are you talking about!" demanded the prisoner angrily.

"Man alive, I wish you could see your face!"

Three minutes later a sailor halted at the door, looked at Truax, then wheeled about to the marine.

"Say, what ails that man? What's the matter with his face?"

"Don't know. Looks fearful, doesn't he?"

"Awful! Ought to have the doctor."

Sam shifted uneasily.

Five minutes later a sailor wearing on one sleeve the Red Cross of the hospital squad came along.

"Say," said the marine, "I wish you'd look at the feller in the brig."

The hospital man showed his face at the grating and looked at Truax keenly.

"Wow! The sawbones officer has got to look at this chap!"

Sam Truax sprang to his feet, but his legs wobbled. He felt his heart-beats racing and his face flushing.

"I felt all right a little while ago, but I certainly feel queer now," he muttered.

Doctor McCrea soon hurried below.

"Sentry, unlock the door! Let me in there!"

Doctor McCrea made a brief examination.

"How long have you been feeling ill?"

"N-not long," faltered Truax.

"Hospital man!" called Doctor McCrea.

"Aye, aye, sir!"

"Have the stretcher brought here at once."

"Aye, aye, sir!"

The stretcher was brought, and the attendants put Truax on it.

"I can walk, Doctor," he protested feebly.

"Can't risk it! To the 'sick bay,' men."

"What's wrong, Doctor?" Truax asked, when he was lifted from the stretcher and placed in one of the berths.

"Don't talk, my man. Just lie quietly and let us get you on your feet - if we can," he added under his breath, but not so softly but that Sam Truax heard him.

The attendant came with a glass of liquid.

"Drink this," ordered the surgeon, "and in a few minutes you'll feel better."

"I - I feel awful," Truax groaned.

The dose was repeated, but the patient continued to grow worse. His nausea was overwhelming and he vomited over and over. In an interval of quiet the doctor leaned over him.

"Have you anything on your mind, man? Any wrong you'd like to set straight before - before -"

A look of fright came into Truax's eyes.

"Doctor, I - I wonder if Jack Benson would come to see me?"

"I'll see," replied the doctor, rising and leaving the "sick bay."

Ten minutes later the naval surgeon returned with Benson. Hal Hastings, Mr. Mayhew and Ensign Trahern followed Jack and the doctor.

"Here's Mr. Benson, Truax," announced Doctor McCrea. "If there's anything you wish to confess, the rest of us can bear witness and help straighten matters out if you've done any wrong that you now regret."

Sam Truax feebly stretched out a hand that was hot and dry.

"Benson, will you give me your hand?"

"Certainly."

"Can you ever forgive me?" moaned the man.

"Why, what have you done?" asked Jack.

"That assault back in Dunhaven -"

"Was it you who knocked me out there?" demanded Benson sharply.

"Yes." In a shaking voice Truax confessed the details of the affair and from that passed to Jack's trip to the suburbs of Annapolis.

"I found the mulatto in a low den. I told him you carried a lot of money and that he could have it all if he'd decoy you somewhere, keep you all night, and send you back to the Naval Academy looking like a tramp." He then added the name of the mulatto.

"But why have you done this?" demanded Jack. "What have you against me?"

"I didn't do it on my own account. I did it for Tip Gaynor, a salesman for Sidenham."

"The Sidenham Submarine Company?" cried Jack, deeply interested. "The Sidenham people are our nearest competitors in the submarine business!" he exclaimed.

"Yes; and they wanted to get the business away from the Pollard Company. They told Tip Gaynor it would be worth ten thousand dollars to him for each Sidenham boat he could sell to the Government. Tip hired me -"

"One moment, please," interrupted Jack. "Did the Sidenham officials know that Gaynor intended to use such methods?"

"I don't believe they did," replied Truax.

"Humph! So Gaynor hired you to do all you could to disgrace me in the eyes of the naval authorities and to injure the machinery in the engine room of the submarine!"

"Yes. Tip said it was highly important that the Pollard boats should break down while under the eyes of all Annapolis, so that it would seem that they could not be depended upon."

Truax here became so ill that his audience had to wait until he could proceed. Then Jack asked:

"What sort of looking fellow is Gaynor?"

"He was the black-bearded man who shanghaied you in the white knockabout. He doesn't usually wear a beard. He grew it for the occasion."

"So, acting for Tip Gaynor, you undertook to ruin us all and the good name of our boats! You even met Dave Pollard and got him to take you on as a machinist for our boats!"

"Tip knew a man who was willing to introduce me to Mr. Pollard."

"It was like kindly, unsuspicious Dave Pollard to be taken in by a rascal like that," muttered Jack to himself.

Sam Truax added a few more details to his confession, then said:

"I couldn't die without telling you this, Benson. I hope you forgive me."

Before Jack Benson could reply Lieutenant Commander Mayhew stepped forward.

"Truax, have you told us the exact truth?"

"I have."

"You thought it would be easy to get the better of a boy like Benson, I suppose."

"Easy enough," admitted Sam. "So did Tip."

"You shot far below the mark in guessing at Benson's ingenuity and brains," remarked Doctor McCrea, laughing. "It was he who suggested this way of inducing you to make this confession after you had refused to answer the lieutenant commander's questions."

"What?" demanded Truax harshly.

"When I was first called in to you, you were not sick, only scared by the remarks of others. After we got you in here, we dosed you with ipecac. That started your stomach to moving up and down."

"What? You poisoned me?"

"The ipecac was my choice. It isn't poison. The general idea was Captain Benson's. With a lad like him you haven't a chance."

"Benson, you infernal cheat, you!" muttered Truax, and started to get out of the berth. But he was weak, and the attendant had no difficulty in thrusting him back.

"In view of what you've been telling us, you'd better not sprinkle bad names about," said the surgeon, turning on his heel. He was followed by the others, all chuckling.

"Mr. Benson," said Doctor McCrea, when the party was in the cabin, "are you my friend?"

"I certainly am, sir," cried Jack warmly.

"Thank you," said the doctor, making a comical face. "With your head for doing things, Mr. Benson, I feel safer with your friendship than I should if I had your enmity."

While they were still chatting in the cabin of the gunboat a shot sounded on deck. Then a corporal of marines rushed in, saluting.

"The prisoner, Truax, sir, escaped while walking under guard on deck. He dived headlong, sir. The marine guard fired after him through the darkness, sir. The officer of the deck sends his compliments, sir, and wants to know if Truax is to be pursued in a small boat."

"At once, and with all diligence," ordered the lieutenant commander.

Though a thorough search was made, Truax was not found. It was thought that the fellow had been drowned. But months later it was learned that he was skulking in Europe with Tip Gaynor, who had received word in time to make his escape also.

For two days more the instruction continued at sea. Then, the tour of instruction over, the little flotilla returned to the Academy at Annapolis. From there Captain Benson wired Mr. Farnum for further orders. Without delay came back the dispatch:

"Navy Department requests that for present 'Farnum' be left at Annapolis. You and crew return by rail when ready."

Soon after this Jack was informed that the Annapolis police had run down the mulatto who had decoyed the young submarine skipper on that memorable night. Jack's money, watch and other valuables were later recovered and returned to him.

Just before Jack and his mates were to leave the "Farnum" for the last time, Lieutenant Commander Mayhew came aboard, followed by Ensign Trahern and three of the midshipmen who had been under submarine instruction.

"Mr. Benson and gentlemen," said Mr. Mayhew, "I shall not make a set speech. What I have to say is that the cadet midshipmen who have been under your capable and much-prized instruction of late wish each of you to take away a slight memento of your stay here."

Machinist Williamson had not been omitted. Each of the four received from the lieutenant commander a small box, each containing a small gold shield. In the center was the coat of arms of the United States Naval Academy. At the top of each pin was the name of the one to whom it was given. Across the bottom were the words:

FROM THE
BATTALION OF NAVAL CADETS
IN KEEN APPRECIATION
OF ADMIRABLE INSTRUCTION

"I think," said Mr. Mayhew, "that none of you will hesitate to wear this pin on vest or coat lapel. The gift is a simple one, but it practically makes you honorary members of the United States Navy of the future, and I am glad of it."

Choose from Thousands of 1stWorldLibrary Classics By

A. M. Barnard
Ada Leverson
Adolphus William Ward
Aesop
Agatha Christie
Alexander Aaronsohn
Alexander Kielland
Alexandre Dumas
Alfred Gatty
Alfred Ollivant
Alice Duer Miller
Alice Turner Curtis
Alice Dunbar
Allen Chapman
Ambrose Bierce
Amelia E. Barr
Amory H. Bradford
Andrew Lang
Andrew McFarland Davis
Andy Adams
Anna Alice Chapin
Anna Sewell
Annie Besant
Annie Hamilton Donnell
Annie Payson Call
Annie Roe Carr
Annonaymous
Anton Chekhov
Arnold Bennett
Arthur Conan Doyle
Arthur M. Winfield
Arthur Ransome
Arthur Schnitzler
Atticus
B.H. Baden-Powell
B. M. Bower
B. C. Chatterjee
Baroness Emmuska Orczy
Baroness Orczy
Basil King
Bayard Taylor
Ben Macomber
Bertha Muzzy Bower
Bjornstjerne Bjornson
Booth Tarkington
Boyd Cable
Bram Stoker
C. Collodi
C. E. Orr

C. M. Ingleby
Carolyn Wells
Catherine Parr Traill
Charles A. Eastman
Charles Amory Beach
Charles Dickens
Charles Dudley Warner
Charles Farrar Browne
Charles Ives
Charles Kingsley
Charles Klein
Charles Hanson Towne
Charles Lathrop Pack
Charles Romyn Dake
Charles Whibley
Charles Willing Beale
Charlotte M. Braeme
Charlotte M. Yonge
Charlotte Perkins Stetson
Clair W. Hayes
Clarence Day Jr.
Clarence E. Mulford
Clemence Housman
Confucius
Coningsby Dawson
Cornelis DeWitt Wilcox
Cyril Burleigh
D. H. Lawrence
Daniel Defoe
David Garnett
Dinah Craik
Don Carlos Janes
Donald Keyhoe
Dorothy Kilner
Dougan Clark
Douglas Fairbanks
E. Nesbit
E.P.Roe
E. Phillips Oppenheim
Earl Barnes
Edgar Rice Burroughs
Edith Van Dyne
Edith Wharton
Edward Everett Hale
Edward J. O'Biren
Edward S. Ellis
Edwin L. Arnold
Eleanor Atkins
Eliot Gregory

Elizabeth Gaskell
Elizabeth McCracken
Elizabeth Von Arnim
Ellem Key
Emerson Hough
Emilie F. Carlen
Emily Dickinson
Enid Bagnold
Enilor Macartney Lane
Erasmus W. Jones
Ernie Howard Pie
Ethel May Dell
Ethel Turner
Ethel Watts Mumford
Eugenie Foa
Eugene Wood
Eustace Hale Ball
Evelyn Everett-green
Everard Cotes
F. H. Cheley
F. J. Cross
F. Marion Crawford
Federick Austin Ogg
Ferdinand Ossendowski
Francis Bacon
Francis Darwin
Frances Hodgson Burnett
Frances Parkinson Keyes
Frank Gee Patchin
Frank Harris
Frank Jewett Mather
Frank L. Packard
Frank V. Webster
Frederic Stewart Isham
Frederick Trevor Hill
Frederick Winslow Taylor
Friedrich Kerst
Friedrich Nietzsche
Fyodor Dostoyevsky
G.A. Henty
G.K. Chesterton
Gabrielle E. Jackson
Garrett P. Serviss
Gaston Leroux
George A. Warren
George Ade
Geroge Bernard Shaw
George Durston
George Ebers

George Eliot
George Gissing
George MacDonald
George Meredith
George Orwell
George Sylvester Viereck
George Tucker
George W. Cable
George Wharton James
Gertrude Atherton
Gordon Casserly
Grace E. King
Grace Gallatin
Grace Greenwood
Grant Allen
Guillermo A. Sherwell
Gulielma Zollinger
Gustav Flaubert
H. A. Cody
H. B. Irving
H.C. Bailey
H. G. Wells
H. H. Munro
H. Irving Hancock
H. Rider Haggard
H. W. C. Davis
Haldeman Julius
Hall Caine
Hamilton Wright Mabie
Hans Christian Andersen
Harold Avery
Harold McGrath
Harriet Beecher Stowe
Harry Castlemon
Harry Coghill
Harry Houidini
Hayden Carruth
Helent Hunt Jackson
Helen Nicolay
Hendrik Conscience
Hendy David Thoreau
Henri Barbusse
Henrik Ibsen
Henry Adams
Henry Ford
Henry Frost
Henry James
Henry Jones Ford
Henry Seton Merriman
Henry W Longfellow
Herbert A. Giles

Herbert Carter
Herbert N. Casson
Herman Hesse
Hildegard G. Frey
Homer
Honore De Balzac
Horace B. Day
Horace Walpole
Horatio Alger Jr.
Howard Pyle
Howard R. Garis
Hugh Lofting
Hugh Walpole
Humphry Ward
Ian Maclaren
Inez Haynes Gillmore
Irving Bacheller
Isabel Hornibrook
Israel Abrahams
Ivan Turgenev
J.G.Austin
J. Henri Fabre
J. M. Barrie
J. Macdonald Oxley
J. S. Fletcher
J. S. Knowles
J. Storer Clouston
Jack London
Jacob Abbott
James Allen
James Andrews
James Baldwin
James Branch Cabell
James DeMille
James Joyce
James Lane Allen
James Lane Allen
James Oliver Curwood
James Oppenheim
James Otis
James R. Driscoll
Jane Austen
Jane L. Stewart
Janet Aldridge
Jens Peter Jacobsen
Jerome K. Jerome
John Burroughs
John Cournos
John F. Kennedy
John Gay
John Glasworthy

John Habberton
John Joy Bell
John Kendrick Bangs
John Milton
John Philip Sousa
Jonas Lauritz Idemil Lie
Jonathan Swift
Joseph A. Altsheler
Joseph Carey
Joseph Conrad
Joseph E. Badger Jr
Joseph Hergesheimer
Joseph Jacobs
Jules Vernes
Julian Hawthrone
Julie A Lippmann
Justin Huntly McCarthy
Kakuzo Okakura
Kenneth Grahame
Kenneth McGaffey
Kate Langley Bosher
Kate Langley Bosher
Katherine Cecil Thurston
Katherine Stokes
L. A. Abbot
L. T. Meade
L. Frank Baum
Latta Griswold
Laura Dent Crane
Laura Lee Hope
Laurence Housman
Lawrence Beasley
Leo Tolstoy
Leonid Andreyev
Lewis Carroll
Lewis Sperry Chafer
Lilian Bell
Lloyd Osbourne
Louis Hughes
Louis Tracy
Louisa May Alcott
Lucy Fitch Perkins
Lucy Maud Montgomery
Luther Benson
Lydia Miller Middleton
Lyndon Orr
M. Corvus
M. H. Adams
Margaret E. Sangster
Margret Howth
Margaret Vandercook

Margret Penrose
Maria Edgeworth
Maria Thompson Daviess
Mariano Azuela
Marion Polk Angellotti
Mark Overton
Mark Twain
Mary Austin
Mary Catherine Crowley
Mary Cole
Mary Hastings Bradley
Mary Roberts Rinehart
Mary Rowlandson
M. Wollstonecraft Shelley
Maud Lindsay
Max Beerbohm
Myra Kelly
Nathaniel Hawthrone
Nicolo Machiavelli
O. F. Walton
Oscar Wilde
Owen Johnson
P.G. Wodehouse
Paul and Mabel Thorne
Paul G. Tomlinson
Paul Severing
Percy Brebner
Peter B. Kyne
Plato
R. Derby Holmes
R. L. Stevenson
R. S. Ball
Rabindranath Tagore
Rahul Alvares
Ralph Bonehill
Ralph Henry Barbour
Ralph Victor
Ralph Waldo Emmerson
Rene Descartes
Rex Beach

Rex E. Beach
Richard Harding Davis
Richard Jefferies
Richard Le Gallienne
Robert Barr
Robert Frost
Robert Gordon Anderson
Robert L. Drake
Robert Lansing
Robert Lynd
Robert Michael Ballantyne
Robert W. Chambers
Rosa Nouchette Carey
Rudyard Kipling
Samuel B. Allison
Samuel Hopkins Adams
Sarah Bernhardt
Sarah C. Hallowell
Selma Lagerlof
Sherwood Anderson
Sigmund Freud
Standish O'Grady
Stanley Weyman
Stella Benson
Stella M. Francis
Stephen Crane
Stewart Edward White
Stijn Streuvels
Swami Abhedananda
Swami Parmananda
T. S. Ackland
T. S. Arthur
The Princess Der Ling
Thomas A. Janvier
Thomas A Kempis
Thomas Anderton
Thomas Bailey Aldrich
Thomas Bulfinch
Thomas De Quincey
Thomas Dixon

Thomas H. Huxley
Thomas Hardy
Thomas More
Thornton W. Burgess
U. S. Grant
Valentine Williams
Various Authors
Vaughan Kester
Victor Appleton
Victoria Cross
Virginia Woolf
Wadsworth Camp
Walter Camp
Walter Scott
Washington Irving
Wilbur Lawton
Wilkie Collins
Willa Cather
Willard F. Baker
William Dean Howells
William le Queux
W. Makepeace Thackeray
William W. Walter
William Shakespeare
Winston Churchill
Yei Theodora Ozaki
Yogi Ramacharaka
Young E. Allison
Zane Grey

www.ingramcontent.com/pod-product-compliance
Lightning Source LLC
Chambersburg PA
CBHW020503100426
42813CB00030B/3097/J